# In Praise of *In Capable Arms*

"*In Capable Arms* is a refreshingly honest, beautiful story. It's a must-read for any who have felt inadequate, like they weren't 'enough.' And it's a reminder that God can use anything—even our most painful situations—to bring about something beautiful. Sarah's book will make you laugh and make you cry, so grab a tissue."

—Lindsey Bell, author of *Searching for Sanity*, a parenting devotion to be released soon; minister's wife and mother of two squirrely boys and four babies in heaven

"Sarah Kovac says every life is a story worth telling, and in her deeply moving memoir she tells her remarkable story very well. I've known Sarah most of her life, and I've constantly been amazed at how the limited use of her arms has set virtually no limit on what she can do. To the list of things Sarah can do without her arms we can now add this: write a very fine book! *In Capable Arms* is a poignant mix of pain and joy, struggle and hope. It's a delightful book to read because it's a compelling story well-told, and it's a book worth reading because how Sarah has faced her challenges is how we should all face our own challenges."

—Brian Zahnd, Lead Pastor, Word of Life Church, St. Joseph, Missouri, author of *Unconditional?* and *Beauty Will Save the World*

"Sarah Kovac challenges us to look our insecurities and struggles in the eye and to know that not even our scariest flaws can keep us from God's love. Sarah's story will speak to each of us, no matter where we are in our journey of life."

—Erin Smalley, national speaker, author of *Grown Up Girlfriends*, coauthor and cofounder of marriage ministry with husband, Greg Smalley, at Focus on the Family

"Wow! I read, *In Capable Arms*, by Sarah Kovac, in one sitting. I couldn't put it down. No longer will my inadequacies define me or stop me but rather point me toward God where true worth and purpose are found. Sarah's story will captivate you, challenge you, and inspire you to be all God created you to be—flaws and all."

—Micca Campbell, national speaker and author of *An Untroubled Heart*

"Sarah's honest account of adapting to a life of limited usage of her arms is incredibly motivating and inspirational. In addition, it is also comforting, exciting, and reassuring to read the proof of a loving God who cares for us even when we are in the midst of really hard stuff. I loved reading about Sarah's relentless pursuit of living a life of normalcy despite what others might have told her as well as the story of her pregnancy and the birth of her sweet son. It's all simply further proof of God's mercy and love not just for Sarah but for us all."

—Natalie Snapp, author of *Heart Sisters: Creating Love and Support Between Women*, to be released by Abingdon Press in 2014

"In her book, *In Capable Arms*, Sarah Kovac takes readers on her own captivating and compelling story of how she overcame adversity and refused to allow her physical limitations to define her. *In Capable Arms* is an inspiring story of faith and triumph that will help readers identify their own fears, insecurities, and limitations and be challenged to courageously overcome them as they discover that God is faithful even when life is hard."

—Stephanie Shott, popular Bible teacher, author, and founder of The M.O.M. Initiative, a ministry devoted to helping the body of Christ make mentoring missional

"*In Capable Arms* is a story of tenacity, courage, struggle, gratitude, and hope—and it's a story for everyone, because as author Sarah Kovac writes, 'Everyone's a mess, and everyone needs grace and help.' Kovac's story is captivating and quickly becomes a just-one-more-chapter kind of read. Readers will find themselves identifying with Sarah in unexpected and delightful, thought-provoking ways. Through it all she gently leans into God's truths and urges readers to do the same."

—Vicki Tiede, speaker, author of *When Your Husband's Addicted to Pornography*

"Sarah's life is a powerful reminder to us all, 'With God, all things are possible.'

Every person touched by a disability can learn valuable lessons from this beautiful woman and her family. More importantly, society's views of people with a handicap will be positively altered after reading *In Capable Arms*."

—Ann Joyner, special needs mother and advocate

"For any of us who have been touched by disability, telling our story can be a powerful, liberating experience. But when telling our story also points our readers to the grace and sufficiency of God, our struggles are transformed into a life-giving testimony. Thank you, Sarah, for allowing your struggles to point to the True North—the God who is capable!"

—Sharon C. Hensley, author of *Homeschooling Children with Special Needs*

# SARAH KOVAC

# IN CAPABLE ARMS

*Living a
Life Embraced
by Grace*

Abingdon Press
NASHVILLE

IN CAPABLE ARMS
LIVING A LIFE EMBRACED BY GRACE

**Library of Congress Cataloging-in-Publication Data**

Kovac, Sarah.
    In capable arms : living a life embraced by grace / Sarah Kovac.
    pages cm
    ISBN 978-1-4267-5695-5 (alk. paper)
    1. Christian women—Religious life. 2. Mothers—Religious life. 3. People with disabilities—Religious life. 4. Parents with disabilities—Religious life. I. Title.
BV4527.K68 2013
248.8′643—dc23

2013008321

Scripture quotations unless noted otherwise are from the Common English Bible. Copyright © 2011 by the Common English Bible. All rights reserved. Used by permission. www.CommonEnglishBible.com.

Scripture quotations marked NLT are taken from the *Holy Bible*, New Living Translation, copyright © 1996, 2004, 2007. Used by permission of Tyndale House Publishers, Inc., Carol Stream, Illinois 60188. All rights reserved.

Scripture quotations marked "NKJV™" are taken from the New King James Version®. Copyright © 1982 by Thomas Nelson, Inc. Used by permission. All rights reserved.

13 14 15 16 17 18 19 20 21 22—10 9 8 7 6 5 4 3 2 1

MANUFACTURED IN THE UNITED STATES OF AMERICA

For Adam, Ethan, and Taylor.

You give me a story worth telling.

# CONTENTS

# CHAPTER 1

# RISK AND REWARD

Because of both my hurdles and my life accomplishments, people seem to think I am a very determined person—that I don't think twice about taking a risk. That once I set my sights on something, I just go for it with no thought to the possible difficulties I may encounter on the way.

Truth be told, I don't see myself as the fearless risk-taker. In fact, nearly every action I take in a day is the result of careful calculation.

I was born with a condition called Arthrogryposis Multiplex Congenita (which means "crooked joints"), a rare congenital defect that left my shoulders, arms, and fingers shortened and lacking muscle. My arms, which are unable to bend, are too weak to do much, and their shriveled, unattractive appearance only adds insult to injury, but they are good for a little light lifting and door-opening when need be. For anything that requires dexterity, I have to rely on my feet.

I face the same maddening struggles over and over—and will for the rest of my life. Think about the most common things: restaurant sandwiches, for one. Because their size is usually unwieldy and they easily fall apart, they are a risk I am generally unwilling to take, no matter how badly I want turkey and avocado on whole wheat. At stop lights I usually lower my foot from my steering wheel so people won't stare. I often hesitate at the tops of staircases, because I fear tripping, falling, and not being able to catch myself. And if there's a fly buzzing around my head, I can't swat it away. I always need to think through my actions, guessing at what might be possible for me and what might not. I spend my days weighing my options and exercising caution.

And yet amid that caution and struggle, there is grace. Grace, and places of rest and opening, places of transformation.

My story is full of pain, fear, and insecurity. I share it with you not so you'll pity me or thank your lucky stars that your life is different. No, I share my story because I've discovered that pain doesn't have to have the last word. There are many ways in which I feel I'm not enough, and that's OK. I don't have to be enough. If I were enough, I would have no need for other people and no need for God. My need keeps me connected to all the important things.

> *And yet amid that caution and struggle, there is grace. Grace, and places of rest and opening, places of transformation.*

I am sharing this with you because I know I'm not alone in feeling inadequate. I'm not the only one who mourns a great loss.

I don't know what your loss is. Maybe, like me, you or someone you love has a physical limitation. Or maybe you are plagued by loneliness. Or maybe you have simply come to a season in your life where something feels persistently *off*. Whatever prompts those voices in your head that say *I'm not good enough*, I hope you will send those voices to the spa for a few hours and dwell with me in a different claim: the claim that our limitations and feelings of inadequacy can actually be the wellspring of our spiritual lives. They can point us to God.

✤ ✤ ✤

Sometimes, bars have been lowered for me and people have expected less of me because of my "crooked joints." I have received pats on the back that I didn't deserve, and I've been denied the chance to earn others. As a little girl I saw this double standard and didn't know how to feel. When would I know I'd done my best? Was there an honest scale anywhere I could use to measure my accomplishments? Over time, I would learn to define risk and achievement in my own terms so that the days I first put on a necklace and cast a fishing pole for myself are some of my proudest memories. I learned to accept accolades with a smile, but I also learned to remember that I was the only one who really knew whether I was doing something worth applauding.

But perhaps the biggest risk I've ever had to calculate was having a baby.

When my husband and I first shared the news that we would soon be parents, the reactions from our friends and family ranged from glee to great concern. Some were of the opinion that I could do anything, and caring for a baby would be no problem for me. Some asked unending questions, as if I'd figured out all of motherhood before I'd even tried it. And some hurt me deeply in assuming I'd rely on my husband to handle all the ways in which they believed I'd be incapable as a mother. I had never doubted my ability to be a good mother until I was being asked all these questions and even being told outright what I couldn't do. I found myself yet again wondering what I really could accomplish, how to measure a "good" mother, and whether I had what it took to be one. Those who believed I could do anything were wrong, but so were the people who expected so little. Was this a risk or an achievement? I could only shut out the feedback and allow time to tell.

When Ethan was born, my legs—with which I intended to stabilize my son in my unstable arms—shook so badly that they were of no use. I had refused the epidural, fearing my lower body would be too numb to handle the baby, but with trembling legs, I didn't even attempt to hold him. Instead, my husband steadied the newborn on my chest. This was, without a doubt, my finest moment. I'd had the natural birth I wanted. I knew I'd done my very best. In this experience in which so many women participate, I was on a level playing field. The bar had not been lowered. The pain and effort had not been lessened for me because I have a disability. I achieved as much as every other woman who's achieved motherhood. It was beyond intoxicating. But the thrill of my victory began to wane as

I realized how badly I wanted to wrap my son up tightly in my arms. Of course they lay limp—as always. All I could do was offer the child as much as he offered me: presence, nearness, wonder.

*But in motherhood and in life, I've learned (albeit slowly) that God created us as community creatures. I wasn't meant to do this alone, and we are designed to lean on each other.*

I looked with a hurricane of emotion into the face of this tiny miracle perched on top of me. Fear jolted through me as I wondered whether I was capable. I wondered whether the doubters were right. Would I end up relying on everyone else to raise this child? What if he grows to resent me because I don't care for him like other mothers do? Would I be enough? What if I fail?

*What if I fail at this?*

My mother, my cheerleader in life, stood by, waiting patiently to hold her first grandchild. The joy of the moment continued to well up in her eyes and I couldn't understand why, with all these things I felt, I wasn't crying too.

She finally held him, all cocooned-up in a blanket and cap. She nestled him in her arms, tight and secure . . . just like I'd longed to. It dawned on me that I would never hold him as gently as she could. I would never run my fingers through his hair when he was sick. I would never hug him tightly or squeeze his shoulder or pat him on the back. I would not be for him the mother she had been for me. What did I even have to offer? I suddenly felt very small.

As my son was eventually passed around to all those who'd made the 1 a.m., hour-long hospital trip, I saw the way he was cradled and cuddled in arms that *weren't* mine. When he was finally handed back to me, I almost pitied him. But there, snuggled beside me with the bed rail and blankets holding him close, I realized that Ethan wasn't worried. He was at home.

As his mother, I feel a huge responsibility to be everything he needs. My mind is constantly guessing at what he might want next. But in motherhood and in life, I've learned (albeit slowly) that God created us as community creatures. I wasn't meant to do this alone, and we are *designed* to lean on each other. The ability to ask for help is a great strength—one I would begin to develop for the first time as Ethan grew. I would not always be everything Ethan needed. God would put many different people in Ethan's life to serve many different purposes. I was just one.

My mother returned the next day to visit us again. I was feeling more confident and though I hadn't been able to sleep because of the adrenaline, I felt rested and full of joy when she arrived. It was almost indescribable, the sense of pride I felt in providing a grandchild, who was the first on both sides of the family. How beautiful, seeing my son cradled in the same arms that had held me. His head pressed against the same heartbeat that had calmed me from conception. My mother, another of the beautiful people who would fill up this boy's life.

Sometimes, when I look at my mother and my son, I remember that things did not have to turn out this well. Out of fear, I could have chosen not to become a mother. And, stepping back a generation, my own mother could very easily have chosen, out of a different set of fears, not to give birth to me. She was an eighteen-year-old art major who lived with her boyfriend and worked at a fast-food restaurant to pay the bills when she got pregnant. A close relative first suggested an abortion to my mother; nobody wanted to see her throw her future away. When my mom presented the option to my dad, he simply left the decision to her and offered his support either way. The only reservation he had about terminating the pregnancy was that he wasn't sure how they could scrape up the money to pay for it. After weeks of deliberation, however, she decided to take the hard road.

As I've been told the story, all through the pregnancy, my mother could be found sitting with a book perched on her ever-growing tummy, reading aloud to the little life growing inside her. Sometimes it was poetry, sometimes nursery rhymes, and sometimes (for good measure) mathematical equations. Other times she could be found lying on the floor with her stomach close to the stereo letting the baby listen to music—sometimes classical, sometimes jazz, and a lot of times Daddy's favorite, Crosby, Stills, and Nash.

My parents decided the best thing to do would be to get married, but as those nine months wore on, my mother wasn't sure they had what it took to care for a child. More than once she toyed with the idea of going to the clinic and calling the whole thing off. But she did not give in to her fear and on October 25, 1983, I was born. Sometimes I wonder what I was doing in those moments as my parents decided whether or not I was worth the effort, worth the sacrifice. But as it was, one girl made an apparently random decision to do the most difficult thing, and here I am typing my story out into a book (yes, with my toes), feeling like I have something to say. And here you are reading it. Her one difficult decision is touching your life even now.

Today, I think about my teenaged parents with the "disabled" young daughter, and I feel in awe of the challenges they faced and surmounted. And when I think back on my childhood and adolescence, I am, frankly, sometimes stunned that I got through the loneliness and isolation and the sheer physical challenges that I experienced as a kid.

As you read my story, I hope that you will not be afraid

to revisit those difficult times in your own life. Remember the times you've endured the unbearable and the times you've managed to summon more courage than you thought you had. Could it be that you were resting on the strength of another?

CHAPTER 2

# FINDING A WAY

The wait was over. The grueling hours of labor passed and my parents looked into the little face they'd been anticipating when all present realized something was terribly wrong. Doctors examined me right away and came back with the report: "It is likely that your daughter is mentally retarded." The young couple tried to grasp what they were hearing. "She will probably never speak, see, or care for herself." No doubt the doctor broke the news as gently as possible to my confused parents, but how does one deal with news like that? Even though my mom didn't believe in God at that time, God was the only one she could think to cry to. *You've made a mistake!* she thought. How could an all-knowing God place this child in the care of two people who were barely making their own marriage work? Their lives were messes separately. Together, it was mayhem . . . and now they had a baby with special needs. Surely God was confused.

The day after I was born, we were transferred an hour away to a larger hospital so I could undergo extensive testing. My exhausted parents heard good news one minute, bad news the next. I was kept in the neonatal intensive care unit while the doctors ran enough tests to be sure what they were dealing with. My parents recall that the nurses at the hospital especially enjoyed my stay in the NICU, as I was one of the few babies they could hold and interact with. I wasn't "sick" in the way that many of the other babies were. Finally, the brain scans came back. To my parents' relief, the results were normal. My eyesight and hearing tested fine. And there was nothing wrong with my brain.

However, there was something wrong with my arms: the doctors explained that my condition was called Arthrogryposis Multiplex Congenita (a few years later, I

would be very proud when I could rattle this off for curious strangers), also known as AMC. Those affected by
AMC show symptoms of locked joints and underdeveloped muscle, often in all four limbs, can have clubbed
feet, scoliosis, and a host of other complications. My case,
fortunately, was an unusually mild
one, affecting only my arms.
However, those two limbs were
hit hard. They would hang limp
and underdeveloped at my sides
for the rest of my life.

> *"God only gives special children to special people."*

Now that my parents had a diagnosis and began to
understand its implications, they headed home with me.
The specialist prescribed that my parents do an unrea-
sonable amount of painful stretching exercises with me
every day, knowing that they would not be able to keep
up the regimen. The logic, the specialist admitted later,
was that if my parents were asked to do what was
humanly impossible, they would push themselves to do as
much as *was* possible.

The first night I was home, I cried nonstop. They were
up all night trying to calm me, but nothing worked. That
is, until 6 a.m., when they decided to play good old
Crosby, Stills, and Nash (something to calm *their* jangled
nerves). The familiar sound put me to sleep right away.

The guilt of perceived failure set in, and as predicted,

my parents found the amount of therapy prescribed to be too heavy a burden. It was hard enough being new parents and not knowing how to best care for me, considering my differences from the average newborn. Picking up their peacefully sleeping baby girl and bending my stiffened joints until I was screaming in pain for *hours* a day was too much. They did the therapy with me for a few hours a day at most. I can remember doing it into early childhood.

Not long after my birth, our little family moved in with my Grandma Grace. My father's mother lived close to the hospital where we'd be spending a lot of time for my physical therapy. She opened up her home rather than have us drive an hour for every appointment. The conditions weren't ideal; I slept in a drawer lined with blankets and Grandma Grace couldn't stand to be around when my parents would start up the daily therapy sessions with me. She couldn't watch me (or them) suffer. But the time spent in her home wound up being therapy for all of us.

*It is important for us to have the space to push ourselves, the space to fail, the space to find our limits while in the care of supportive parents and family.*

Back in 1983, my parents couldn't get on the computer and find a forum for parents of children with AMC. They didn't have access to websites for information and support. They felt utterly alone in their struggles and were unable to find any real connections with other families to encourage them. They could never be sure if they were giving me too much freedom, or not enough. Would I benefit from more adaptive equipment, or should I be left to adjust to the world as I am? Should I be encouraged to use my hands more, or allowed to use my feet? As my parents wrestled with feelings of inadequacy and fear of the future, Grandma Grace's calming presence and steady faith proved to be the healing balm they desperately needed. She had raised my father in a Christian home, and though he didn't claim any faith during my infancy, she quietly reminded my parents that, "God only gives special children to special people." Her confidence was just enough reassurance to pull them through.

My precious Grandma Grace passed away a few years ago, but her wisdom resonates in me, even as I raise my own son. Her words proved true with my parents; though they felt inadequate, they were the perfect parents for me. I know that God knew me before he formed me in my mother's womb and God knew Ethan before he formed him in mine.

> You are the one who created my innermost parts;
> you knit me together while I was still in my
> mother's womb. (Psalm 139:13)

Before I created you in the womb I knew you;
before you were born I set you apart.
(Jeremiah 1:5)

God chose me to be this boy's mother, and what I'm doing now is no surprise to God. So I never need to fear that I am not enough (though I will always fight the natural tendency to do so).

Never knowing how far to push me or how far they should let me push myself, my parents found raising me a difficult balancing act. Every new parent looks for help when wondering what the next milestone should be and when their child should reach it. But my mom and dad couldn't be sure when I would become mobile. They had no clue when or if I would begin to feed myself, learn to write, or even how I would do any of those things. Because I couldn't pull things to my face to chew on them like babies do, I went around putting my mouth *on* household objects to explore them. And because my hands are turned under, I couldn't crawl. Instead, I rolled

*Journal:* In what situations do you most frequently find yourself questioning your "enough-ness"? Is there a common thread between these situations? Something in your past or your family? How can we give these moments into God's care instead of feeling we have to be it all?

around like a little log and usually stopped rolling under the swivel rocker. I would roll until the top half of my body was under the chair, and then just lie there, staring at the maze of metal rods and connectors. Later, I learned to scoot around on my bottom before learning to walk at the average age. I started figuring out how to eat with my feet around age two-and-a-half.

My parents let me problem-solve and adapt to situations. Sometimes it took years. I remember being around ten years old and calling my mom because I had buttoned my pants using my hands for the first time. I was so excited to tell her that I called her at work. Any buttoning I'd done previously was using an adaptive tool called a buttonhook. I generally avoided adaptive tools and was excited to be free of that one. Ironically, this is the only tool I still use on occasion. I admire the way my parents stepped back and let me *be* in my slow, not-always-logical way. More than once I was offered suggestions on how to do things faster and easier, but sometimes those were not the choices I was ready to make. I needed the validation of finding my own way and finding success in it.

I fumbled my way through pretty much every normal kid activity, with my parents standing supportively nearby. Their help was readily available but never forced on me. I believe this is huge for the emotional health of a child with a disability. It is important for us to have the space to push ourselves, the space to fail, the space to find our limits while in the care of supportive parents and family. Given the opportunity to do this frequently at a young age, as we grow up, we begin to know ourselves and become comfortable with our limits. The better we know our limits, the easier it is to foresee the challenges any situation may hold.

If I can know the challenges I will face, I can prepare and be more likely to walk away happy with how I adapted. People need a chance to find out what they're made of. We need to know if we have what it takes. We need people who believe in us and who see a failure only as a minor setback instead of a game changer. How else can we find confidence?

Because my parents allowed me to test myself so thoroughly early on, I approach most situations with confidence. As I type this, I am about to embark on my first solo traveling experience. I will be flying to another part of the country; I will be dealing with security checks and a layover each way, checking into two different hotels, and catching two different shuttles. My parents and husband will be worried about me, that's a given. My mom even offered to accompany me. But,

> *We need people who believe in us and who see a failure only as a minor setback instead of a game changer.*

there's something about traveling alone that, in my mind, has always represented the ultimate step of independence.

My parents taught me that I may have a disability, but I'm not "disabled." Not one of us is perfect. And that's OK. What's *not* OK is letting our flaws define us. It is not OK to use our challenges as excuses to keep us from becoming the people God wants us to be. This is the wisdom I hope to pass to my son. I want Ethan to grow up knowing that he is loved and accepted no matter what he does or does not do; no matter how he succeeds or fails. He is defined neither by his accomplishments nor his weaknesses. I want him to know that who he *is* runs deeper than skin, deeper than flaws and strengths, deeper than achievements. He is God's child, he is our child, and he is loved. No matter what. In fact, it's become our little game to echo back and forth our love by saying, "I love you! SO much! Forever and ever! No matter WHAT!" By the time Ethan is repeating back the, "No matter what!" he is usually yelling and throwing his hands in the air for added emphasis.

❖ ❖ ❖

From where I sit now, it seems that the fact that our family is even together is nothing short of miraculous. My parents were so young when I was laid in their arms.

They were so far from "ready." But God had a beautiful plan for them. My parents were not perfect and they've told me many times that there are things they would go back and change if they could. But the older I get, the more amazed I am at the flood of grace that God unleashed on our little family from the very beginning. The number of times we *should* have fallen apart, or never come together, is a testament not only to God's goodness to us, but also His faithfulness to answer the prayers of my Grandma Grace.

From my first breath, I breathed grace. It was God's goodness that my parents chose to wrap me up in their arms that brisk October morning, imperfect as I was; imperfect as they were. Who but God could know how well we could function as a family with Him at the center? My parents weren't searching for God, but he was near to us. By God's great mercy, I knew nothing but the security and warmth of a loving family. That security caused this little girl to believe that anything was possible—even without the use of hands.

*Journal:* Take a few minutes and look back. Can you see all the ways in which your life might not have been? What did it take for this day, this grace, to happen?

# CHAPTER 3

# ONE OF THESE THINGS IS
# NOT LIKE THE OTHERS

Today, many are concerned about political correct-
ness. Nobody wants to use the wrong terminology
and offend somebody. Are we disabled? Persons with disabilities? Differently abled? The term I grew up with was
*handicapped*. Being labeled anything at all made me
cringe. It was a long time before I was able to come to

terms with the fact that the world runs on labels and biases simply to keep things and people categorized, not usually out of cruelty. When someone describes me to a stranger, I am not so naive as to think the first thing they mention is my distinctive nose or the color of my hair. No, the most easily identifiable quality about me is my arms and the fact that I eat and drive with my feet. I choose not to be insulted that I am recognized this way; it's the quickest way to pick me out of a crowd.

But for many years, I denied I was different from anyone else. I tried so hard to blind others with my chipper personality or with achievements in hopes that these would become my defining qualities. To an extent, it worked. In taking chipperness to an extreme, I once was described as "too zany" by a boy I had a crush on. Whoops. What I didn't realize was that I was neck-deep in denial; what counselors understand as the first of five stages of grief.

It may seem strange to hear me say that I have grieved over this congenital disability. After all, how can you mourn something you never had in the first place? I believe that there are things in life that we instinctively know should be. There have been many, many times when it has surprised me that I wasn't able to do something with my arms. It was as if my brain expected my arms to function as well as anyone else's and then remembered they couldn't. I sometimes dream that I have no disability. How on earth can my subconscious even envision that? Often, in conversation, I will find myself saying I'm going to do something with my hands, when I will really do it with my feet (such as, "I'm going to wash my hands for dinner"). It's as though, after all this time, my brain is still trying to catch on to the fact that my hands really don't work.

It has taken me many years to begin to see the benefits of the grieving I've worked through. I don't kid myself to imagine that I will have ever "arrived," or that I will ever, on this earth, be at perfect peace with my imperfect body. However, allowing myself to really mourn my loss has brought me to a much healthier place—a place where I feel I have something of value to contribute—not in spite of, but in the *midst* of my weakness.

I wonder how many people with disabilities (or other "lost" things) do not recognize their need to grieve. I

*Journal:* What loss have you suffered? A loss of a dream? A job? A loved one? Something physical in nature? Have you allowed yourself to grieve? Which stages of grief have you experienced (denial, anger, bargaining, depression, acceptance)? Looking back over your life, can you notice signs that you might have been grieving over something?

wonder how many are in a stage of grief and don't even know it, or even know why they feel so depressed or angry?

✦ ✦ ✦

Being a little girl and trying to understand where I fit in the world, denying my differences was a natural place to begin. As I tried new things and experienced all I could, sometimes I was proving to myself and others that I could do it—that I was no different. And, sometimes, I was just a little girl having fun.

But having fun meant challenges. My mom's heart must have jumped straight up into her throat that first time I had roller skates on. As soon as she'd tied the laces and helped me stand, my feet rolled right out from under me and I landed on my rear. I have a long string of vivid memories of firsts such as roller skating. It makes me wonder who displayed more bravery: the girl with the skates or the parents watching.

It was to be a bravery tested again and again during my childhood. We have all lost count, but at least seven times my parents had to rush me to be put back together after I'd fallen on arms that broke under my weight. The joints in my arms didn't bend much, so if I fell on them, my frail bones could do nothing but snap. I broke my left arm four times during my first-grade year. That arm took all the abuse because my left elbow bent less than my right, so if I fell on both arms, my right arm would bend while the left broke. The worst break, however, came during my freshman year of high school when I broke my right arm into three pieces. It took four hours of surgery, four pins inserted into the bone, and a wire wrapped around the joint to put me back together that time. The little mobility I'd had in my elbow was lost with that break and now both arms are equally stiff. If I fall again, I'm not sure what will happen. I'd rather not find out.

I remember being stuck in bed often in my early childhood. There were not only broken arms but also tonsils that tended to swell enough to block my entire airway. On several occasions I was rushed to the hospital gasping for air. When I'd broken an arm, I had to deal with the pain, the cast, and the nauseating medications, but recovering from breathing problems had its own set of challenges. After several trips to the hospital, the doctor told my parents that they could care for me at home if they assembled a makeshift breathing tent like the hospital's, creating an environment of moist, cool air. My parents set up a series of trash bags over my bed to keep the air from the humidifier in. I can remember hearing

*How many are in a stage of grief and don't even know it.*

people come to visit, but I couldn't leave my bed to talk to them. My parents, however, would come and sit in my muggy little tent with me, as I was lying in there, miserable, sticky, and bored.

Outside was the place I wanted to be. Where my dad would catch fireflies for me in the garden and put their "light" parts on my finger as a ring before I realized how gross that was. Outside, where my parents watched me careen down the driveway for the first time without training wheels. I was scared to use the brakes, so I just tipped over in the patch of grass at the bottom. Outside were my neighborhood friends, playing in sprinklers, drawing cities in chalk. And here I was, in this dumb tent.

My breathing issues eventually subsided, and as I learned to watch my step more carefully, I found that I spent far less time cooped up in the house.

❖ ❖ ❖

I didn't understand why I was different, or why other people felt the need to stare, but I was a happy little girl. I especially loved animals (they never seem to notice just how different I am, and they certainly don't stare). I named all the neighborhood cats and talked my parents into adopting strays on more than one occasion. Once, I lured a shepherd-mix dog into our yard with a peanut butter and jelly sandwich. Another time, after having responded to a salvation altar call at school chapel, I led my cat, Sox, in a lengthy, heartfelt salvation prayer. I explained to her why she needed Jesus in her life, asked her to repeat after me, and paused to allow time after each phrase for her to repeat it to herself.

When I wasn't proselytizing the family pets, I attended a faith-based school, where I was asked to pick out my favorite Bible verse. I selected Philippians 4:13: "I can do all things through Christ who strengthens me" (NKJV). In elementary school, I interpreted and applied that scripture to my life in the only way I knew how. I took that to mean that God would help me do anything I set my mind to, be anything I wanted to be, and conquer any obstacle. Now that I'm older, I no longer interpret the scripture this way, but I imagine it's healthy for children to believe they have unlimited potential.

The things that God has called me to do, God will strengthen me to do. However, many times I've been faced with the fact that, no, I cannot do all things just because I want to. One of my earlier revelations of this was in church. My parents started attending church when I was two and I remember at some point feeling confused when the pastor asked us all to lift our hands to God in worship. At first, I lifted my hands as much as I could—about six inches out from my side. During the next service, I thought God might like it better if I sat in the pew and lifted my foot to him instead, since I could lift my foot straight up. Then I realized that the difference in altitude reached between the foot and hand was probably not much different, considering I sat when I raised my foot. I felt less like I was participating when sitting, so I figured God would be OK with my six-inch hand-raise. I clearly remember this being a serious dilemma in my mind. I so badly wanted to participate to the fullest. I wanted God to see my hands lifted with all the others.

*The things that God has called me to do, God will strengthen me to do.*

Today, there are times in worship when my arms almost ache to lift themselves in an act of surrender. I cannot help but feel a disconnect as I awkwardly pass the offering bucket along, the music ends, and hundreds around me clap while I can only smile my approval or limply tap my hands together. I want to join in that sound. When the moment comes to greet those around us, I'd love to shake hands with confidence; but as it is, I never know if they will draw their hand away and pat me on the shoulder, or apologize as they grab my wrist, because they didn't know what to do. After twenty-six years of being part of the church, it is still a struggle for me, because society is a struggle for me. But I keep going back, and finding joy there. It's where I belong.

I have no doubt that as long as there are *people* making up the body of Christ (hint: forever) this imperfect person will run into uncomfortable situations, painful moments, people I don't like, and people who don't like me. Church leaders will make mistakes and church members will make mistakes. Everyone God works through is entirely human, and just as human are the hands that God chooses to use in my life . . . should I reject them because of their imperfection and awkwardness? God chooses to use my imperfect hands as well.

✦ ✦ ✦

"Raise your hand if you want to be Sarah's bathroom buddy."

It was 1987. I was four years old, and any time I had to use the restroom, I relied on girls in my kindergarten class at the Christian school to volunteer to help me unbutton and rebutton my pants. I wasn't old enough yet to be embarrassed that I needed assistance using the bathroom. After all, my classmates also tied my shoes for me, helped me put on my coat and even wrote my name on the board for me as punishment when I was in trouble. I instead saw it as a unique opportunity to escape from class with a friend.

Over time, the amount of help I needed lessened. My mom discovered she could sew fabric loops into the inside of an elastic waistband. I could hook my crooked fingers into these loops and, by yanking from my shoulders, pull them up on my own. We bought shoes I could slip on and off, I figured out how to don a coat by using my mouth, and I learned I could write on the chalkboard by holding the chalk with one foot and balancing on the other. (Much to my dismay, though, in the 1990s I never did figure out how to tuck in a shirt or "wave" my bangs.)

My world was one giant question mark. I expected to do the same things as every other kid, but if asked how, exactly, I wouldn't have had an answer. I found ways to play four square, dodge ball, and even softball with everyone else, but I had to find my own way. I couldn't throw a ball or hold a bat in the same way as the other kids, but because my dad had taken the time to play Wiffle ball with me in the summer, I was ready for recess softball when school was in session.

One of my favorite memories is of Dad and me playing Wiffle ball in the front yard. I had graduated from the wide, red bat to the skinny yellow one, which I wound my curved right arm around. I held on to the bottom of the bat with my left hand and in my mind, I looked just as good as any Royals designated hitter. Dad hid the ball in his imaginary glove, refused two suggestions from the imaginary catcher, finally nodded, and lobbed the ball to me. I fouled it into "right field," under the apple tree. My opponent recovered it and we repeated the dance, except this time I felt a hard "thunk" when my bat connected with the ball. Dad had pitched me an apple. Giddy, I insisted he pitch the apple to me several more times. I couldn't hit it far, but it gave me a taste for hitting a real softball, which I would do at school later on. Much like the Wiffle bat, I've had to take the time to find my own grip on the world. I had to wrap my arms around it; I had to get comfortable with how it felt in a controlled, safe environment where I wasn't afraid to fail. It prepared me to take a swing when the harder, heavier things came flying at me.

My home was an oasis, of sorts. I was safe there. Our house had a large yard dotted with fruit trees. In the back was a magnolia— its accommodating branches stretched out low so I could say

*"Maybe God doesn't heal me because by not healing me, God can help a lot more people."*

there was one tree in the world I could climb (when my parents weren't looking). This same magnolia blossomed in the spring right outside my bedroom window, so on warm Missouri mornings it was as if God set the world's most fragrant bouquet in front of my waking eyes. Down the hill was my dad's large vegetable garden, where he let me help plant the seeds. I would plop down in the freshly-churned soil, poke out little divots with my toe, and gingerly lay the seeds to grow.

When my parents took me out in public, I noticed people looking at me funny. I knew I was different. And I hated it. I couldn't understand why, of all the kids I knew, I was the one who so often had to watch from the sidelines—unable to participate in the activity of the day.

There was no one, nothing to blame. Arthrogryposis occurs in only one of every three thousand live births. But I was the statistic, the one out of three thousand kids.

*Why me?*

We've all asked that question at some point (likely many points) in our lives. Why me? Why would God allow this to happen? Why am I being asked to bear this? Where are my answers? We live these "lives of quiet desperation," as Henry David Thoreau put it. We feel the injustice, but don't want to trouble anyone else with our pain.

Growing up, I felt like maybe I should be feeling something, saying something about my pain, but I wasn't sure *what* I felt or where to direct that emotion. I didn't think anyone would understand me even if I did figure it out. I tried not to pity myself or talk about my frustration. Instead, I tried to blend in and held on to hope that things would change . . . that God would do something miraculous.

I clearly remember sitting in the passenger seat of my mom's car. We were driving home from a Friday night church service. Whoever had been preaching that night had called for people who wanted prayer for physical healing to come forward at the end of the service. I had been prayed over many times, but I walked to the front once more, full of faith and anticipation that this was the time that God would *God worked to heal those things in me which I didn't even know were broken.* send me home "whole." After the prayer, I walked back to my seat, paying extra close attention to how my arms felt. Nothing out of the ordinary. I tried to hold on to my faith a little longer. But once again, I felt embarrassed after the church service, knowing all those people saw me walk away from the prayer having my request denied. I felt as if I had failed somehow.

As I sat in the car, staring at the moon, a thought occurred to me that sparked a new, different kind of hope in my heart. I turned and said, "Mom, maybe God doesn't heal me because by not healing me, God can help a lot more people."

I do *not* believe God caused me to be this way. James 1:17 says, "Every good gift, every perfect gift, comes from above. These gifts come down from the Father, the creator of the heavenly lights, in whose character there is no change at all." Jesus confirms good gifts and a loving God in Matthew 7:9-11: "Who among you will give your children a stone when they ask for bread? Or give them a snake when they ask for fish? If you who are evil know how to give good gifts to your children, how much more will your heavenly Father give good things to those who ask him." God is a good Father, and one who can accomplish his will without giving little Emma cancer or Aunt Carla Alzheimer's. Pain and suffering are in the world because sin disrupted the harmony God intended.

I have come to understand I was born with a disability because I was born into a world shot through by sin. And yes, I also believe God could heal me if he chose to; but instead, God has caused something painful to transform into a source of joy. God knew how to work through my imperfect life and knew what fulfillment I would receive through it. God knew healing my broken body would do nothing for my broken spirit and set to work on my broken spirit instead.

A disability truly is a *loss* to be *grieved*. In fact, in writing this book, I've come to the realization that in coming to terms with my disability, I have journeyed through all five stages of grief: denial, anger, bargaining, depression, and finally acceptance. Some stages were out of order, and most took me many years to work through. What I do know is that through each stage and my circumstances, God worked to heal those things in me which I didn't even know were broken.

As I began to accept that my life was different, I started to see that God had a purpose for my life, for just who I was. I also understood that having a sense of purpose in life doesn't take the pain away; it only gives us a reason to push through it.

It has always been a struggle knowing how to interact with people who are unfamiliar with my differences. Some want to ask me all sorts of questions, and some are so uncomfortable they don't look me in the eye. As a child, I once laid it all out by introducing myself to a stranger in this way, "Hi! Do you know me? My arms don't work." I found I was much more comfortable discussing it than hearing whispers at the next table over or feeling the stares from across the room.

My young friends often forgot my disability. I remember occasions when they handed me toys or suggested games I

*Journal:* What are current struggles or a painful past that you can see God using to help others? Begin here: Could you be an encouragement to someone going through a similar situation?

couldn't use or play just because they thought of me as "normal." However, one day I was at a friend's house playing when she let me have a turn at the computer. I started to put my feet up to the keyboard (just like I'm typing now) and she said, "Gross! Don't put your feet on the desk!" I remember feeling surprised and embarrassed that someone would be disgusted by my feet. I would learn my friend wasn't alone in the sentiment. As a teenager, I was asked by the staff to take my feet off the table at a pizza joint, my leg was once swatted to the floor by a passing server at another establishment, and I've been asked not to touch the serving utensils at a buffet I liked to frequent. The thought that some people are disgusted by my feet is a tough one to swallow—after all, my feet probably have fewer germs on them than the average pair of hands—my feet aren't touching grocery carts and public door handles. But people's issues with feet aren't generally something that can be debated away. I just have to deal with the knowledge that some people are grossed out by the way I live, even though I wouldn't live like this if I had the choice.

When I was around thirteen, my mom started a group for disabled teens with an organization called United Cerebral Palsy where she took me for regular meetings. They all seemed like very nice kids to me, but I didn't feel I had anything in common with them, even though we all had disabilities. I know I would've benefited greatly from having friends who understood the struggles I faced because life really was a very different place for me than for any of my able-bodied friends. That left me feeling very misunderstood at times. My father said to me once, "Sarah, you aren't disabled. You have a disability." I took that lesson to heart at a very young age, but only now am I learning to turn that truth outward and unlabel the disabled around me. They aren't disabled. They are people. People who happen to have disabilities. When I was younger, I only thought, "I am not them. I am not like those handicapped people." Of course, I knew I wasn't like the able-bodied people either, so I was left to wonder where I fit. How ironic that I only saw people as being arranged neatly under their respective banners, therefore making it impossible for me feel at home with any of them. I knew I had depth. I knew I defied labels. I just didn't realize the same was true for them too.

*Only now am I learning to turn the truth outward and unlabel the disabled around me.*

As my childhood drew to a close, I left behind much of the physical brokenness I had endured. The arm breaks would become less frequent, and the breathing problems disappeared. I would carry with me, however, a love of music, art, and writing. The arts would serve as a much needed release valve for my emotions.

Yet even as my physical body began to break less, something in my spirit began to crumble. The upcoming years would be difficult and often dark. In feeling so different, I found myself becoming more and more isolated. As a teenager, I began to slide deeper into depression, until I finally found myself wondering if people around me might be less burdened if I were gone.

Throughout my adolescence, these feelings of despair—feelings of being overwhelmed by the challenges of youth on top of the challenges of a physical limitation—would come and go. When they arrived, they threatened to never leave, but eventually some incarnation of grace—a word from a friend or a calm moment hiding in the magnolia tree—would remind me of goodness.

Even now, I know these difficult feelings hover at the door, and I sometimes fear that they will barge in and take over. But what I know now is that even if the feelings do return, I can wait them out, and, indeed, pain that appears to be despairing and murderous may actually contain—if I listen very carefully—a grace note of hope or consolation from God.

# CHAPTER 4

# PERFECTION VS. BEAUTY

My alarm always went off three hours before we'd have to embark on our thirty-minute country drive to school in town. I wasn't getting up so early because I had to feed the chickens or bail hay, or whatever it is farmers do in the morning. No, my father was a salesman who worked in the city selling copy machines, my mother worked with him, and our little house was home only to us three humans, two dogs, a cat, and my crested canary named Ringo. I awoke with three hours to spare not to spend time in prayer or reading my Bible or even to cook breakfast. I never had time for breakfast. The only thing that could cause this groggy junior high girl to peel herself out of bed before the dawn was, you guessed it, junior high *boys*.

*I thought that if I worked hard enough, if I could be perfect enough, someone would see me as beautiful.*

The girls at school did their makeup perfectly, their clothes fit perfectly, and their hair fell perfectly. I attended a private school, where many of the students in my small class came from affluent families and were able to buy the right shoes, the right jackets, and the right jeans. I don't know exactly how much my parents sacrificed to send me to that school, but I know that tuition was a struggle. And we certainly didn't have spare money to purchase name-brand clothes that I would outgrow in a year.

I can remember being on the playground when a female classmate chided, "Sarah, you need some different jeans. Your behind just kind of melts into your thighs." In my surprise and embarrassment, I could only muster an angry sneer in reply.

And then at the water fountain, a boy noticed my off-brand shoes. "Where did you get those, Walmart?" He immediately pointed out my uncool footwear to the rest of the class. I managed to laugh along as if it didn't sting. Even if we had been able to afford the brand-name apparel, I had difficulty with zippers and buttons and clasps and ties. My options were very limited. (News flash to the girl on the playground: if your only option had been baggy jeans with an elastic waistband, your backside might not have looked so great, either.)

I couldn't help wearing awkward-looking clothes at that point in my life, but I could control how my hair and makeup looked, and that is why I would allow myself three hours to get ready every morning—and still managed to run late. I hadn't figured out yet how to simultaneously brush and blow-dry my shoulder-length hair, so instead I brushed it out, picked up the blow dryer with my foot and directed the air back and forth until I started to notice tangles, brushed the rats out, and repeated this process until it was dry. It took forever. By the time I was done, every strand curled under *perfectly*.

On to makeup. As I was still learning the art, I was constantly making mistakes, despite the care with which I held the mascara wand between my toes, or the steadiness of my foot while I drew on eyeliner. I would accidentally smudge my mascara or extend eyeliner too far or get foundation in my eye. Less than *perfection* was not an option, so I would wipe the area clean and try again.

And I chose to do all this using the magnified, lighted side of the mirror, so I could be sure to see every little imperfection. Obsessive? Yes. Oh, but junior high boys are *so* worth it, right?

I thought that if I worked hard enough, if I could be perfect enough, someone would see me as beautiful. *Someone? Anyone? Does anyone see how perfect I am? How symmetrical my eyeliner is? I was working on this before the sun was up! Hello?*

Despite my countless hours of primping and preening, my appearance wasn't more than mediocre. Perhaps if I'd stopped inspecting myself so closely through the magnifying mirror and stepped back to take in the whole picture, I would have seen ways to make noticeable improvements instead of microscopic ones. My vision had tunneled down to the point that I only saw rebellious strands of hair instead of the way my hairdo was framing my face. I was critiquing parts of me only I would notice.

I used to take pride in this tunnel-vision, perfectionist tendency. The irony was, of course, that the more I insisted on things being perfect, the less things were anywhere close to perfection. I would look at my messy room and be so overwhelmed by all the little details that would need to be set right that I would decide I didn't have the time or the energy to do it right then. Time would pass, and my room would only become more chaotic. Finally, there would come one day when I decided that I did indeed have the energy and time to do it "right," and I would take an entire day to clean one (disgusting) room.

The French philosopher Voltaire said, "The perfect is the enemy of the good." I thought that I needed to be achieving perfection, and because I bought that lie, I didn't even bother to attempt the good. Perfectionism is something we wink at, as if somehow despite the disabling effect it can have on one's emotions, it is endearing and cute. We claim with pride that we are perfectionists and things have to be "just so," or we are unhinged. Now, I believe in a certain amount of order. I believe structure, discipline, and excellence are things to strive for, and I'm working on implementing more of those into my life.

But there's a difference between having order and not being able to welcome people into my home because it's not perfectly clean. Or being late to work because my hair refused to cooperate. Or missing a special experience with my son because I am in the middle of a project and don't want to stop.

*Journal:* Where do you tend to get so caught up in the details that you miss the big picture?

These moments are not cute. My perfectionism is not cute. It is often nothing but an excuse for poorly ordered priorities. Would I really rather be alone than let people in on the truth that (the horror!) my house is messy sometimes (OK, often)? Maybe my priorities are out of whack. Maybe I'm valuing my pride more than the relationship. Maybe if I'd rather fuss with my hair than be punctual, I'm valuing my appearance over others' time or money, whichever the case may be. Perfectionism is a pride thing. So not cute.

*The more I insisted on things being perfect, the less things were anywhere close to perfection.*

The only way I've been able to find genuine growth in these areas has been to begin seeing that my character is simply the sum of my decisions. I've tried to think of the person I'd like to be and just acted like that person with this decision in front of me, whatever it is. If kindness is an area in which I'd like to grow, I challenge myself, not to be a "kind person," but to be kind at this moment.

I've been known to write character goals on my to-do list for the day, set reminders on my phone, and motivate myself with my computer's wallpaper. If I choose differently one day at a time, act like the person I want to be decision after decision, pretty soon I'm not acting. If I can continually ask myself, "Can I love *this* person? Can

I tell the truth right now? Can I make a responsible choice just for today?" in time, my choices will align with my desire for change. The math will start adding up to someone different. The future blooms from the seeds of now.

In the dysfunction of my perfectionism, I wasn't planting. I was only trying to survive in the jungle I'd allowed to grow out of control around me. I saw the chasm that stood between who I was and the girl I wanted to be—the girl I knew I *should* be—and I gave up without a real attempt to change. It seemed impossible. It was easier to blame God for creating me that way: awkward, bitter, and justifiably so. It was God's fault wasn't it? Shouldn't God be the one to fix it?

✦ ✦ ✦

In junior high my only real priority was acceptance. I wasn't concerned with my character; I wanted to fit in, like every other junior high school student on the planet. I wanted to be popular. I wanted my opinion to matter. I wanted to be smart and talented and pretty. I wanted to be perfect. Boy, was that not in the cards. I was told that I was talented when it came to the arts and creative writing, but as to the popularity, and fitting in, it wasn't going to happen.

All through elementary school, I'd been painfully shy. Ever the quiet one, I would rarely speak up when I knew the answer in class (out of a paralyzing fear that I could be wrong) or ask other kids to play (afraid they might say no, or worse, say yes out of obligation). Instead, I waited to be called on for the answer or asked by the other kids if I'd like to join them. As social pressure mounted in junior high school, this tactic wasn't working so well. I found myself alone quite a bit or spending my time talking with the teachers, who always made me much more comfortable than kids my age. A bright spot appeared when my parents and grandfather invented a contraption that made it possible for me to play the trumpet in the school band. My trumpet was held up to my face by blocks of wood, which were secured to a desk chair using C-clamps. Popsicle sticks were glued to the valves, and to those sticks were tied strings which could be pulled by pedals at my feet. So, when I pushed a pedal, a corresponding valve was pulled down. Since I am "right-footed," I worked two

*Journal:* What are places in your life where you wish to see genuine growth? Character traits? Virtues like kindness? Charity? Faith? What are current decisions and upcoming ones in which you can act with kindness or faith in the moment.

valves with my right foot, and the third pedal with my left. The invention was later improved to use bicycle brake cables instead of strings and was altered so that I could use it in any chair, not just a desk chair. It was pretty creative. God knew what he was doing when he gave me an artist for a mother (who had the idea), a musician for a father (who helped perfect the design), and an electrician for a grandfather (who built it).

Music afforded me a place to feel like I excelled.

"Sarah, how would you like to play with the high school band for the Christmas concert this year?" my band teacher asked after my junior high band practice.

"Are you serious? Yes!" I practically squealed my response to such an honor. My mom tells me that several audience members cried when I played "O, Holy Night" for my very first solo.

When I played, I could express what I could not in words or visual art, though I loved those other media as well. My favorite pieces to play were the slow, emotive, soulful movements (preferably in a minor key, perhaps 6/8 time) with which I could expose the more wounded places of my heart without anyone really knowing it. I felt my strength as a player was my ability (need) to pour my soul into the performance. Music gave me a much needed outlet. Still, my interest in classical instruments wasn't a great boon to my social life. Music did offer me a refuge where I felt comfortable and excelled, but on the broader stage of junior high school society, I was becoming more isolated.

I became convinced that the popular girls hated me. I was rarely invited to their parties outside of school or to gatherings during the school day. I was, of course, the stereotypical "last one picked" for most team games, with the exception of kickball, where everyone expected me to have a miraculously strong kicking leg. I disappointed my team consistently on that point.

The one or two girls who were kind enough to run around with me would abandon me for the in-crowd given the chance. I didn't understand what was so inherently different between them and me. I was intensely jealous and began to feel bitter toward women in general, and even my own femininity. I began to despise all things "girly." If I was so lucky as to be invited to a sleepover, I would decline—surely it would be nothing but one big estrogenfest (a waste of time, I thought). I disliked wearing pink and would've rather gouged my eyes out than don a pair of tights. On rare occasions, I would dress up and enjoy wearing something frilly, but those days were few and far between. We're talking years between.

This gender-specific anger was easy to adopt, as the group at school consistently nice to me was the boys (I am defining "nice" very loosely here). I've always had an interest in football and cars, so conversation with the guys always flowed much easier. We had more in common. I was good enough to be their friend.

I no longer wanted to be just "one of the boys," but the girls wouldn't have me. Yet again I found myself feeling as though I was some alien creature that didn't *really* fit anywhere. I have never been much of an actress, and my bitterness, jealousy, and general gloominess began to seep into my relationships with my classmates. No one seemed to see past my lack of popularity to the fact that I was a good person. I was a good person, wasn't I? Maybe I had some rough edges, but didn't I have some redeeming qualities too?

*I've tried to think of the person I'd like to be and just acted like that person with this decision in front of me, whatever it is.*

I remember talking with a friend after class one day, and I said, "I feel like I live in a bubble. Everyone can look at me, but no one will get close enough to touch me."

I still sometimes feel that way. Well-meaning people are so interested in the superficial aspects of my life that they go no further. They ask me how I do things, walk up and watch me like I'm something on display, quiz me on my daily activities, but don't seem to notice that who I am could be even more intriguing than what I do. So many times I am amused by the thought that I'm stuck in a famous person's life, without the benefits of being famous—instead I get only the stares and curiosity and lack of personal space.

Of course, bubble or not, I didn't realize that every other student in my junior high class was feeling similar pressures. We all wanted to be perfect. To be accepted, loved, prized, acknowledged. I didn't know that it was a struggle even for the ones to whom it seemed to come so naturally. I didn't have a clue that the popular girls had problems like the rest of us—like me!—they were just adept at hiding them. I didn't see that even the star athletes were insecure too. All I saw when I looked at these people was *perfection*. But myself I knew much more intimately. I knew my bitterness and insecurities. I knew how often I blabbered like an idiot in front of a cute boy. I knew all the things I wasn't good at. I knew how I looked in a swimsuit. I knew how my arms flopped around when I ran. I knew all these *imperfect* things about myself.

As we all struggled to climb the social ladder, my loneliness only deepened my depression. One day, I found

*Journal:* Have you ever felt the loneliness of "not fitting in" or "not being good enough"? What are the steps to getting out of that feeling? Hint: Blaming others is not step 1.

myself sitting alone during some sort of free activity time. The class had divided itself up to play games. In my insecurity, I couldn't bring myself to ask if I could join a group, and I took the lack of an invitation as a hint that nobody wanted me anyway. I walked out of a classroom door onto a fire escape landing to clear my head. I leaned against the rail and took a deep breath. A few clouds were scattered across an otherwise cheerful sky as I looked over the empty playground below and felt foolish for the tears I was fighting back. My vision had filtered down to only the pain, the isolation, the suspicion that I was merely being tolerated, and the fear that those who were nice to me acted that way out of sympathy for the poor crippled girl. I stared at the black concrete and thought how easy it would be to rid everyone of the burden and annoyance I surely was.

I stepped one foot and then the other onto the bottom of the two rails. I pressed my thighs against the top rail for balance, since my arms were too short to hang on. It would be so easy to relax a few muscles and rid myself of this torture: this day-in, day-out of never-ending proof that I was less-than, that I would never be as perfect as the others. The distant concrete looked very inviting.

Now that someone has called me "Mama," and I know what it is to love my child more than my own life, I cry as I bring this memory to mind.

In my isolation, I distanced myself from people, and their emotions, to the extent that empathy became nearly impossible for me. I'd found that getting close, that loving and hoping for love, was a risky game. I saw no reason to continue letting people break me, so I shut my heart away. I locked it up where it would be safe, and there, without the constant bending and flexing that relationships require, it began to petrify.

So, as I hung hopeless over the fire escape, it wasn't that I didn't care what my family and friends would feel when they lost me. I was simply not aware of it. I only wanted to escape the fire, the torment.

What kept me from doing this was not guilt about how sad my parents would feel or some sort of romantic longing to see one more springtime of flowers. What kept me alive was theology—or, more precisely, fear of God's wrath. I believed that my decision to end my life would not allow me to enter heaven.

*I've seen, though, that the most beautiful and interesting things in the world are imperfect.*

After a great war was waged in my mind, I came to the conclusion that I could live another fifty years in hell if it made possible an eternity in paradise. I don't even know where I stand on this issue now; I don't pretend to have all the answers. However, that thought saved my life despite my anger with God in allowing this pain to go on.

I stepped down from the railing, wiped the tears away, and went back inside feeling foolish and even more alone. No one said anything when I walked back in, and it would be more than a decade before I would tell anyone what happened that day.

I would love to be able to say that I immediately recognized the problem, thawed my emotions out, and became a social butterfly. In reality, however, life went on much the same as it did before. I would continue to steel myself to pain, not realizing that pain has a maturing effect. I wanted to be wise and beautiful, but wisdom and beauty in life are acquired through pain, through tragedy, through surrender to the hurt. In my desperation for a perfect, complication-free life, I was fighting the very things that would bring about beauty.

I would never bloom into a social butterfly. I would never be perfect. I would never be a supermodel. I would never think of the smartest thing to say at the right time (just thirty seconds after). I would never have a flock of guys chasing after me, and I would never be the very *best* at anything. My body had its flaws, my life had its flaws, and that would never change.

I've seen, though, that the most beautiful and interesting things in the world are imperfect as well.

Two years after that moment on the fire escape, I got to go with my church's youth group to Barcelona, Spain. I was totally astounded by the architecture there; hundreds of years old, chiseled by hand, and far from "perfect." But it was the flaws and imperfections that made these buildings so fascinating, so treasured . . . so *beautiful*.

In all of God's creation, there is no one creature exactly the same as something else. Every tree is different. Every fish, every leaf, every hill, every rock is unique. When God looked over all he had made, he said it was *perfect*.

Wait . . .

"God saw everything he had made: it was supremely good" (Genesis 1:31).

The Hebrew definition of the word *good* here speaks to being "pleasant, agreeable to the senses." God created a world that is aesthetically pleasing. He created goodness. That's what you are, and that's what I am. We are pleasing to God, even though we aren't perfect. We are good.

How tempting it is, when our senses are flooded with

*Journal:* In the last 24 hours, have you sacrificed some beauty in your life so you could pursue success, fame, money, etc.? What's one way you can slow down in the next 24 to appreciate more beauty?

images of the life we're supposed to want—the body, the money, the fame—how tempting it is to chase those slippery shadows. To sacrifice beauty in our pursuit of perfection. We don't have time for the scenery when we're careening toward a destination we assume will be worth it. A destination we assume will be there if we can just arrive.

I thought that if I could only be flawless, I would be loved. My life would be whole. If I were less awkward, more gracious, more beautiful, less melancholy, people would find it easier to see the good in me. But in all my scratching and obsessing over perfection, I totally missed all the love that was already in my life. I missed beauty all around me, within me. Instead, I chose to chase my idea of perfection—a pursuit that nearly killed me.

Sometimes, all a girl can do is live one more day, and somehow I managed to just do that. One more breath, one more step.

# CHAPTER 5

# CRUTCHES

With legs that do double-duty, two limbs working as four, I've often wondered what would happen to me if I broke a leg or if my feet developed arthritis from overuse. Crutches wouldn't be an option, as my upper body couldn't support my weight. Thankfully, I've never had to lean on a physical crutch, though I have plenty of experience with emotional ones. I often used my pain as an excuse for why I couldn't change. I didn't believe I could stretch and grow past my differences. But around the time high school began I began to realize just to what extent I'd disabled myself and to what extent I was leaning on excuses and anger. But what was I supposed to do when I constantly hurt? The easiest thing was to shut down.

After I completed the eighth grade, my parents went through a difficult time financially and had no choice but to pull me out of the private school I'd attended since kindergarten. I remember my shock when one day my father turned to me in the passenger seat and asked, "How would you feel about attending a public school the next year?" I stared blankly for a moment, and then burst into tears as I spoke the opposite of what I felt. "I think it will be good. It might be neat to meet new people," I choked through the sobs as I denied my surge of panic. Dad didn't have much of a response to the confused answer I gave, except to say that nothing was for sure yet. The drive home was a quiet one.

*Sometimes even our misery can become so comfortable, so normal, that it's a scary thing to let it go.*

If I was so miserable with life, you'd think I would have been relieved at the thought of change. Still now I struggle to understand it, but I think sometimes even our misery can become so comfortable, so *normal*, that it's a scary thing to let it go. My loneliness was becoming like a warm blanket for me to wrap around myself and hide in. It was all I knew. My situation in life had become my excuse for being angry, closed-off, and sullen. My pain became my identity. Who was I without it? Could I be trusted with a fresh start? Could I bear to open myself up to the hope of new relationships and the possibility of being rejected all over again?

I had become so dependent on my pain and isolation, that I didn't even know how to function without them. I wanted a better life for myself. I wanted to be happy, to have lots of friends, to feel love, but I wasn't willing to change. And I didn't know where to start.

Blaming our problems in life on what is beyond our control relieves us of responsibility to work for better. If we believe ourselves to be nothing more than ocean waves, tossed around by whatever wind happens to come along, then we feel justified in whining and wailing and shaking our fists at God, but we feel no drive to change our own lives.

*Journal:* Are there ways you have overprotected yourself by rejecting others?

Who can change the wind? Though my legs suffered no disability, I was voluntarily walking through life with crutches, and they were rubbing me raw, leaving my ability to give, empathize, and love atrophied.

❖ ❖ ❖

I knew that the winds were shifting, but I was surprised when my parents informed me that in the fall I would not be attending the public school as planned. Instead, I would be homeschooling. We homeschooled for both my freshman and sophomore years of high school, and I found a strong social network that homeschooling families had built in our area. In those two years, I participated in art classes, a production of Shakespeare's *Henry VIII*, a group performance of an Irish step dance routine, and a formal "film review" of *Monty Python and the Holy Grail*, among other activities. Through homeschooling, I met kids who would become lifelong friends. Many of the homeschooling families also attended the same church,

*Journal:* Is something negative so embedded in your life that you can't picture yourself without it? Do you have difficulty imagining a "you" with no anger, depression, unforgiveness, hatred, emotional dependency, and so on?

so there is no shortage of photos of our late-night Bible studies and outdoor acoustic worship services. It was a family.

The people I met during that time didn't seem so preoccupied with social status. Even though I was a newcomer, and obviously different, I was welcomed into the group and felt like I finally fit somewhere. It felt like there were no "cool kids," there was no social ladder to climb. We were all just a bunch of nerds having fun. I think they'd all agree.

With my parents both still working full-time, the academic side of homeschooling proved to be difficult for me since much of my homework had to be finished during the day, by myself. Any questions had to be postponed until they got home in the evenings. It was a lot to ask of an immature, unmotivated teenager to work through the curriculum without much supervision. I was generally scrambling to make up for homework I'd skipped and lessons I'd left incomplete.

After two years, my parents were able to send me back to the structure of the private school, which seemed to be a better fit for us. Having gained confidence and optimism in the time away, I prepared to return to my small class and hoped to start fresh with the other students. Surely we'd all done a lot of growing-up during our freshman and sophomore years. Surely now I would be wanted.

There was very little change in the class roster since my eighth grade graduation, so when I returned, most of the faces were familiar. I was working against my own previously formed opinions of them, and theirs of me. I walked into the building with my head held high and a smile on my face, determined to show everyone how much I'd grown and how fun I could be. My new persona stuck for a few weeks. The girls

*Nobody holds the power to define me, unless I hand it to them.*

were nicer to me than I remembered and the overall attitude was much more kind. But as the first quarter wore on, nobody seemed to have changed much, and the changes I thought I'd undergone seemed to evaporate the moment I settled into the old environment. Eye rolls and sneers and turned backs again filled my days, and questions in my mind of whether I was worthy, wanted, and valuable came flooding back. Clearly, I couldn't change enough to be what they wanted.

When the time of year came for our prom, when all the high school was abuzz with gossip and every girl anxiously waited to be asked, I waited too. No boy in my class had shown interest in me before. Just maybe someone harbored a secret crush? I heard daily news of how So-And-So asked So-And-So. It seemed the single guys would rather go dateless, so I finally broke down and took my best friend from another school (a girl) to my junior prom. A guy friend from church accompanied me to the senior prom. At both proms I had fun, but walked away convinced . . . *I am not enough.*

You know what? It might have been true that some of my classmates didn't enjoy my company. It might have been true that I didn't fit in. But we fall into a trap when concluding this is somehow about our inherent inadequacy. It feels good to be accepted by your peers, but being rejected doesn't mean there's something wrong with you—just like fitting in doesn't mean you've got it all together. Every one of us has issues. Every one of us sins. Every one of us has secrets, wounds, fears, and insecurities. From the billionaire CEO to the prom queen to people like you and me—we all need grace. We all are searching for peace. Don't let anyone fool you. We all have fallen short of what we're intended to be, and if there is good in our lives, it comes from above, not from our own worthiness. Whether I was enough wasn't the issue. I am as imperfect as everyone else, but I am also a child of God. Some high school social assessment of me had nothing to do with my worth as a human being.

Still, a destructive way of thinking took root in my mind, and I began to believe that how people treated me was indeed a reflection of my value. I allowed others to size me up and tell me what I was worth, and sadly, I chose to agree with them. Of course, there were also plenty of positive forces in my life who were sources of encouragement and love. My parents were always letting me know that they believed in me and that I had everything I needed to be anyone I wanted to be. The teachers and staff at my school were life-giving. They made me love my school despite the trouble I had with my classmates—they seemed to "get" me much better than my peers. They didn't coddle me but let me do things my own way. My church and its staff were also a source of positivity. At church I learned how much I was worth in God's eyes, and how people's judgments of me didn't ultimately matter.

Unfortunately, the negative voices stuck with me, the ones telling me something was wrong with me. It would take real faith to believe what God said about me.

*Journal:* Can you identify ways in which outside forces try to determine your worth? These might be loved ones, coworkers, or certainly the mainstream media. Do you feel like you have to be smart/successful/funny/sweet enough to be deemed good enough? What happens when you fall short of the standards imposed on you? Have you ever believed the lie that your "enough-ness" is in any way based on what you do? How did you feel?

The problem was that deep down I didn't feel worthy of love. I felt that not only was I malformed on the outside but there was also something that made me less-than on the inside.

*If I could just be normal, I thought. If I had what God had so generously bestowed on everyone but me, maybe then I would be happy.*

*Maybe then someone special would find me attractive.*

*Maybe then I could fit in.*

*Maybe then people would love me.*

As I write this, I am not even thirty years old yet, but I've become increasingly convinced that twenty-nine is a conundrum. I am still young enough to feel wise, but old enough to know I'm not. With what wisdom I have gleaned, I look back at my high school self, with her excuses and whining, and shake my head. While I try to extend forgiveness to my past, I believe it's also important to examine what I might have done differently so my pain is not wasted. What would I change? As I let go of my past, it is important that I learn from it, or else I will very likely be making those same mistakes again.

It is clear to me now that what I believed to be the source of my problems really wasn't. I oversimplified things. My being different was not the determining factor when it came to my happiness, my relationships, or my confidence. I allowed my disability to become my "whipping boy," blaming it for everything. It was an easy, almost natural, defense against a world that seemed built to isolate me, which was easy because, seriously even the most "accessible" buildings aren't exactly foot-friendly. Nobody's thinking of people like me when they're designing accessible schools or public restrooms. I wasn't even the same as all the other different people! Because I was different, I assumed I must always be seen as different, awkward, socially unacceptable.

I assumed my unhappiness was caused by the one thing I had no control over.

*While I try to extend forgiveness to my past, I believe it's also important to examine what I might have done differently so my pain is not wasted.*

When we are aware that we have, in some way, been shortchanged in life, we suddenly become aware that we have been missing out, that our world is incomplete. We may be without a parent's love. We may have lost someone close. We may never have experienced a stable, peaceful, supportive home life. We may have seen or lived through a traumatic event. We may not have been blessed with a fully functioning body, or our abilities may be slowly leaving us. Whatever it may be, there is loss. We all feel loss at some point, and for many, the worst part isn't the trauma of the loss itself, but slowly coming to terms with the gaping hole it left. "Normal" waits on the other side of a Grand Canyon–sized crater with no clear path to get back to it. It seems almost absurd that the sun would have the audacity to rise in the morning just to highlight your misery, but there it is, waiting for you to begin your long trek through the canyon. This is where we grieve.

✦   ✦   ✦

It's funny, until I started writing this book, I had no idea that I'd ever truly grieved anything. Why would I? I've had it pretty good. I mean, yeah, my arms don't really work, but I was born that way. Why would you grieve something you never had? But when I took the time to examine my past, I saw clear signs of a life spent working through loss. And I asked myself the questions, *Why am I so happy now? What changed in me, or my life, to transform a bitter young lady into a deeply grateful adult?* The answer I found was that I began to scratch the surface of acceptance.

When I recognized acceptance as the turning point in my story, I immediately thought of the stages of grief (acceptance being the fifth), and wondered if I'd journeyed through the other four. If so, it had taken me twenty-five years to begin to touch on acceptance. I was intrigued.

Doing research I found Elisabeth Kübler-Ross's five stages of grief: Denial, Anger, Bargaining, Depression, and Acceptance very easy to identify. However, these stages did not show up neatly and in order. I hopped from one to another, at one point telling God I'd give up sugar forever if he'd heal me (so glad God didn't take me up on that!), becoming angry that he didn't, and then finding some acceptance that I was being ridiculous and God had a plan for me just as I am.

I sat down with a therapist to see if what I'd experienced truly was grief, as opposed to simply learning to live with my differences. After all, my progression through the stages wasn't exactly "progression." It was more like slow wading from one, to another, back to the first, on to the fourth, and so on for a quarter of a century.

"I think I've been grieving," I started slowly, seated cross-legged in the overstuffed chair, "but it's not how I've heard grief described, so I'm not sure."

"Have you done much reading about the grieving process?" she asked, pen and notepad at the ready in her lap.

"No, not much," I admitted.

"That's good," she smiled. "Recent studies have shown that grief is not so much the well-defined process it was believed to be. Most people don't begin with stage 1 of grief and finish with stage 5. It is a lifelong peeling away of many layers, like an onion."

"Do you think it's possible to grieve the loss of something you've never had?" I probed. "For a person like me, there was not necessarily a tragedy or moment of loss. I've never experienced what it is to be physically whole. If I don't really know what I'm missing, can I actually grieve what I lack?"

"Absolutely!" she nodded. "Just think of an orphaned child. They may not have known their biological parents, but you bet they grieve that loss."

Grief is often a lifelong companion in some form. No matter how much acceptance I find, there will always be days when I am not OK with what I've lost. I will never be done grieving. There will be times when the sting of my loss is greater than others. Times when I feel angry and want to scream. Times that I feel thankful for all the good God has brought out of my pain. Times that I would trade anything to hold my son high in the air and see him giggle. That's OK—it's part of the process. As I heal, acceptance will come easier and the painful moments

*Journal:* Have you ever been left feeling powerless/robbed of peace by some event, loss, or other situation that affected you? In retrospect, did you have more control than you thought? What could you have done to at least reclaim a spirit at peace?

will be fewer. There has been loss, and I respect myself enough to allow space for my grief. I will allow myself space to heal.

So, blaming my unhappiness only on a disability was not healthy and was not part of the healing process. As I spent all my mental energy finding creative ways to dump all my sorrows on my disability, I relieved myself of responsibility to change. It's so convenient to transfer all of our problems to that basket and believe it's *all* beyond our control. Even when there is some correlation between our overall happiness and the losses we face, it is a mistake to believe there is nothing we can do to improve our situation . . . even if just a little. Even if it's simply by changing our attitude. Attitude is almost everything.

That I believed my unhappiness to be out of my control further contributed to my unhappiness. Had I realized the power I had to change, the very hope of change would have transformed my outlook completely. But bundling all my miseries together with a disability that wasn't going away left me in despair.

There are events, losses, hurts in life that come along and would define us. They will swallow us whole if we let them. We begin to associate other parts of our life to this one thing, until it's hard to tell where it ends, and we begin. For example, let's say I have been having a lot of headaches lately, so I hop onto WebMD, plug in my symptoms, and pick out the diagnosis that sounds right. Suddenly, I know why I've been irritable, why my eyes have been hurting, why I didn't want to do the dishes last night, why I yelled at the dog, and why I haven't slept. My diagnosis is that I have a virus. Days pass, as does the headache, but to my astonishment, I still don't want to do the dishes, I still yell at the dog, and my eyes still hurt when I've been working for a while. What gives?!

What my diagnosis failed to do is separate what I was *experiencing* from what I was *doing*. There are things we experience that may be painful, but it is important to distinguish those things from that which we *do* that causes us pain. We may not always be able to control what we experience, but we have choices when it comes to the things that we do. Sometimes we fool ourselves into believing that we aren't doing anything to perpetuate painful circumstances.

*It is a mistake to believe there is nothing we can do to improve our situation . . . even if just a little.*

It's more comfortable to believe we are just the victims and there's not a thing we can do. We have experiences that are beyond our control, but we always have a choice in how we react—what we *do*. How we react determines whether we're really a victim or whether we allow our experiences to make us better. I need to grieve my pain, but I don't have to be a victim.

There were many things I endured—*experienced*—in high school that I could not control. From the sports I couldn't participate in, to the clothes I couldn't wear, to the social scene I wasn't part of. But the choices I made —what I *did* in response—only added to the pain I was already experiencing. Thinking I was the victim, I chose a self-protecting "take me or leave me" attitude instead of looking for ways I might be there for someone else. I chose to be cold. These were my choices, and I daresay they caused me much more pain than Arthrogryposis ever could.

So I really shouldn't have been surprised when girls stopped asking me to their parties, or when I didn't have a date to the prom. I told myself it was because they were all shallow and were only interested in being with people who made them look cool, but the reality is that I never gave them much reason to look past my physical flaws. My battle was not against the Big Bad World, but against my own sinful nature, my own negativity, my own bitterness, my Inner Victim. Coming to a place where I do own

*Journal:* Do you ever see yourself as a "victim"? What steps can you take to see yourself differently?

all this, where I have begun to acknowledge the part I've played in my own suffering, has been empowering. As it turns out, the only one with the power to victimize me was *me*. People can hurt me, experiences can wound me, I can feel the sting of loss. But nobody holds the power to define me, unless I hand it to them.

CHAPTER 6

# THE WARS
# WE WAGE

I slunk in and found an open seat near the back of the training room full of unfamiliar faces. An employee handbook lay closed on the table in front of me. I was early for orientation, and as I waited I wanted so badly to flip through the manual to see what would be expected of me at my first job, and I might just peruse the employee benefits section while I was at it. But I sat stiff in my chair. It was too soon to draw attention to myself.

Not long after I'd graduated high school, my dad found that there was a call center hiring in our town, and I was thrilled at the thought of making my own money. I went in during the hiring hours the company had listed, applied, interviewed, and was asked if I wanted to start a few days later. I couldn't believe my luck! I had no previous experience or training, no clue how I would even physically do the job, yet they were eager to have me.

So when orientation day arrived, I was desperate to make a good impression. I wanted the company to be glad they took the risk. I wanted my coworkers to be happy I was there. I was too nervous to do anything but shyly smile at a few other trainees until the supervisor arrived to kick things off. We were asked to open our manuals, and I fumbled with the massive binder with my hands, as I didn't want to use my feet any more than necessary so early in the game. I'd prefer people got the chance to at least hear me speak first, so they would know that my disability was only physical and not mental as well. But all too soon we had to log on to the computers blinking before us, so I slowly leaned back and moved my feet to the desk, being careful not to make eye contact with anyone. There's nothing worse than accidentally catching a stranger in mid-gawk. I'd rather let them compose themselves before I look up again.

We logged on and I was typing away, leaned back in my chair, toes buzzing over the keys. Nobody said a word, and the trainer, the one I *had* to make eye contact with, didn't flinch. Maybe they were warned by HR? Regardless, the day was going smoothly, and I was starting to relax. Our trainer had to leave the room for a bit, and we were left to flip through our manuals or familiarize ourselves more with

*For someone with a disability, the struggle for independence is lifelong.*

the computer system. I was navigating through the scripts on the computer when a loud and irritated voice from the doorway ordered, "GET your feet off the desk!" Of course I knew immediately that this person was speaking to me. He must have thought I was some slacker kid who didn't have enough manners to keep her shoes on and feet off a desk in a place of business. I moved my feet to the ground as my face must have turned twenty shades of red. I was mortified. It reminded me of the time I was asked not to have my feet on the table when I was eating at a pizza joint. I was reminded of the time I was asked not to serve up my own food at the buffet anymore. And when the waitress had smacked my foot off the table as she walked by. I was so ashamed. I felt disgusting. *Do I owe the whole world an apology for the way I am?* I sat with my head down, trying not to cry. Our trainer came back, unaware, and the day went on as planned. And I hated myself.

The next day, our trainer approached me on a break and told me that the supervisor who had reprimanded me didn't know my situation, and of course felt awful. I smiled and acted like it was nothing. Just like every other time someone had left me feeling humiliated. I think I never stood up for myself because, on some level, I felt I deserved to be treated that way. Or maybe just that it would be unfair of me to expect more of people. It was as if, because my arms didn't work, I had been stripped of the basic human right to be regarded with respect by my employer or by business establishments. They weren't offering it, and I certainly wasn't asking for it.

James 4:2 says, "You don't have because you don't ask." When negotiating, it's well-known that if you accept whatever the other party offers first, you're going to get shortchanged. Humiliation after humiliation taught me that this concept holds true in a larger context as well. I was just taking whatever society was offering, and some-times I was being offered, well . . . crap. I thought it was the right thing to just quietly stand there and take it, but come on. No person deserves to be treated that way, and I wasn't doing any favors for the next person with a dis-ability who came to that establishment by acting like it didn't bother me. The fact is, I could have asked. I could have asked to speak with the supervisor who scolded me so we could clear things up. Instead, I accepted a half-apology by way of another person. I could have asked that I be given the right to eat and serve myself at those restaurants, just like every other human who enters. Instead, I just let a wave of shame wash over me; I'd repulsed someone again.

For someone with a disability, the struggle for independence is lifelong. Though we in the United States are profoundly blessed to live under a government that promotes equality and penalizes discrimination, there is certainly no shortage of people who would take one glance at a person like me and make snap judgments about my work ethic, my politics, and whether I contribute anything at all to society. Am I saying that those judgments are always wrong? Of course not. But honestly, you're just as likely to make that snap judgment about an able-bodied person and be correct. For some reason, we tend to make those quick, negative judgments about people who look, dress, and act differently

*Journal:* Where have you experienced someone else's ignorance? When have you judged someone, or been too afraid to ask, to speak, to meet, equal to equal?

than we do. And unfortunately I am "different" from almost everyone's perspective.

Ignorance is not a thing of the past, as anyone deemed "different" can tell you. Webster defines *ignorance* this way: "lack of knowledge, education, or awareness." If you don't know the details about a person, why he or she looks a particular way, or what it's like to be in someone's shoes, you are experiencing ignorance. We all do it, and it is no place from which to make a judgment call about someone. If you are experiencing ignorance, the best thing you can do is make the choice to move away from your ignorance by becoming more aware of that person's experience. If you are not able to talk to the person, then admit that you are experiencing a moment of ignorance and choose not to form any negative thoughts about that person.

Unfortunately, no matter how much we try to spread awareness, promote tolerance, or punish discrimination, I'm afraid we can't completely wipe out ignorance. I know I will forever watch as nervous parents whisk their pointing, curious children out of my periphery. (Why not encourage your child to initiate a conversation with me instead, therefore making me seem more like a person and less like a scary monster? Even better, could you perhaps strike up a conversation with me yourself, so your child can see that you respect me as an equal?) There will always be the gawkers, the disgusted, and the too-afraid-to-ask. It is their choice, and their loss, to stay that way. There is a world of wonderful people they will miss out on, but it is their right to do so.

We, the different, the gawked-at, have our choices too.

I may often be on the receiving end of discrimination, but I am not beyond dealing it out to others. I have to make a conscious decision to learn instead of making assumptions and to remember that just because someone discriminated against me does not make me any more righteous. Awareness and open-mindedness are to be worked for and don't come naturally to any of us. In fact, isn't it true that we are born knowing nothing but our own needs? As we grow, we are taught to share, that we shouldn't bite other kids, and that we have to wait our turn. Later in life, if you were blessed like I was, we are taught about integrity, how to contribute to our families, and how to be respectful. The list could continue, but the point is that we (should) spend much of our young lives being taught that *it's not about us*. There are other people to consider when we bite, refuse to help out, are

*Journal:* Can you see a pattern in the way God speaks to you? How do you respond?

disrespectful, and so on. As we take these lessons to heart, we mature and find we can navigate through society easier.

But these hard lessons do not end when our parents stop teaching us. Remember, we can never know it all (tell that to "high school me"!). There will always be areas of ignorance in our lives, and we have to actively seek them out and work against them.

✤　✤　✤

I've never been one to respond to harsh discipline. Embarrassment and fear only cause me to hide or freeze up. My parents recognized this and wisely pulled me aside to correct me quietly in public or to talk with me about my poor behavior (and punishment) instead of yelling or lecturing at home. Not to say that arguments never escalated as I got older and tempers flared, but my parents knew the most effective discipline for me was the calm, not-embarrassing type, and sometimes it was good to let me explain myself and hear why I was being disciplined.

God knows me more intimately than any person could, but I find that God corrects me in a very similar way. A situation will arise and God whispers in my ear, "Pay attention, Sarah. This is important." God knows what kind of person he created me to be, and he knows I'll take the time to think about what it was I needed to learn from that situation. No embarrassment, no fiery judgment, just His still, small voice and my response to it.

> The LORD said, "Go out and stand at the mountain before the LORD. The LORD is passing by." A very strong wind tore through the mountains and broke apart the stones before the LORD. But the LORD wasn't in the wind. After the wind, there was an earthquake. But the LORD wasn't in the earthquake. After the earthquake, there was a fire. But the LORD wasn't in the fire. After the fire, there was a sound. Thin. Quiet. When Elijah heard it, he wrapped his face in his coat. He went out and stood at the cave's entrance. A voice came to him and said, "Why are you here, Elijah?" (1 Kings 19:11-13)

God is not in the violence, but in the whisper. God doesn't lecture or yell, he just asks a simple question (for the second time in this chapter) to cause something to click for Elijah. Before later giving Elijah instructions on what to *do*, God first wants him to have a revelation. Elijah feels like a failure and has curled up under a tree, begging God to just let him die already. So God sends him hiking to this mountain where, before giving any answers, he twice asks, "Why are you here, Elijah?"

God has the power to manipulate the elements and get my attention, but he doesn't. God could speak to me through a tornado or lightning, but he doesn't. God has yet to drop a blinking, neon light in my yard telling me which way to go. Why? Because God knows me. Perhaps if it were that easy to find Him, I would stop seeking. It's important for me to seek out revelation about who God is, who I am, and *why* I need to change . . . then the change comes more naturally, and deeper, than it would if I were obeying "because God said so."

❖ ❖ ❖

A couple of years after joining the workforce, I would really be on my own for the first time. I packed up all my belongings and moved into a campus dorm. Granted, it was a mere eight minutes from my parents' house, but this was my first real taste of independence.

I shared a suite with an RA (resident advisor) who could be classified as a social butterfly. We became fast friends and she introduced me to what must have been half of the student body. Soon, we were attending parties together regularly, and there always seemed to be some-one visiting our room. Anyone who's spent time on a sec-ular university campus knows how this story goes, and while I stayed away from doing anything illegal, that time was spent working out what I really stood for and what was mere "inherited faith."

Having grown up in a Christian home and having attended a Christian school, living life by biblical stan-dards was all I'd ever known. I'd never even touched alcohol, uttered a curse word, or had my first kiss.

Though, in kindergarten, I did ask my parents' permission to kiss a boy when he was playing at our house. My parents said no. (It's OK, Andrew. Kindergarten-me probably wasn't much of a kisser, anyway.)

When I moved into that dorm, away from my parents' and teachers' supervision, I experienced a kind of freedom I'd never felt. No one expected me to be "good" here. In fact, they didn't seem to expect much of me at all. For the first time in a long time, I felt accepted, wanted, and appreciated by my peers. My roommate and her friends were always inviting me to another party, I was making lots of friends, and I seemed to have found my niche in the journalism department. I was even made editor of the opinions section of the university's newspaper and given my very own desk. Though my time living on campus was certainly not 100 percent wholesome, and my record of good behavior took a major hit, I can look back on this time with gratitude because I walked away with some valuable lessons for the journey.

The time I spent running around from party to party answered a question that had always plagued me. As the ultimate geek in high school, I wondered if I was even capable of fitting in with the "popular girls." But I found that the party life I was so enamored with wasn't as glamorous as I'd once thought. (Vomiting into a bathtub after drinking too much is neither fun nor glamorous.) Fitting into a larger group than my high school class of twenty wasn't as difficult as I expected, and as much as I loved my new friends, I found I wasn't enjoying the fast pace. Though I finally felt like I was succeeding socially, the success was hollow.

At the start, I enjoyed the attention I was getting from the opposite sex. I was straying about as far as possible from what I knew to be right, but I just wanted to feel loved and beautiful—how wrong could that be?

But my loneliness only deepened as the months passed, and the behaviors stayed consistent. One night, I was alone. Utterly alone with my thoughts, my battered heart, my guilt. All this time, I'd been living this life during the week and had the audacity to show up at church to smile at my parents and pastors as if everything was fine. My parents aren't stupid; they knew something was up, but they let me learn my lessons.

That lonely night, a lesson hit me hard. I had built a life of superficial relationships at college. Sure, I had a ton of friends who would meet me at a bar or for a party. There was a list of guys who would come around, but those people were not interested in being there when I needed them. We were all just in this for what we could take from each other. The realization of just how alone I had become in this sea of people was nearly unbearable. I just wanted to be held. I wanted someone close to make me feel safe, but all the strong arms in my phonebook were too busy for me.

Except, I knew there was one guy I could call. It was a little awkward to do it because it was late and we hadn't talked in a while, but I knew he would answer if I called.

To my great relief, he just said, "Sure, come on over."

I drove to my parents' house, where I knew I'd find Dad watching TV at this late hour. At twenty-one years of age, I curled up in his lap like I was two, listened to his heartbeat, and wondered why life gets so complicated. I just wanted to feel loved—was that so much to ask? I'd finally found what I thought I wanted, but the mirage faded and left me even thirstier than before.

I drove back to the campus not quite sure how to feel. I had enjoyed feeling like a child again during that hour next to my dad, but I did have to go back to the reality I'd created for myself. Nothing had changed. I hadn't changed.

That hour with my dad was not entirely unlike prayer. It's easy to fall into the trap of thinking that spending an hour with our Father every so often will fix our problems.

*Journal:* When do you feel driven to change after spending time in God's presence? Does it wear off? Explore the reasons why.

We can go to church every day, but God won't force us to change if we don't really want it. It's comforting to be in God's presence, and we are welcome to crawl back into His lap anytime. But if time spent in God's presence doesn't inspire us to change, to obey, what's the point? Are we just using God like a Band-Aid? Is God nothing more than a momentary distraction from how screwed up things are? Or can we choose to recognize that God walks with us *through* the messes we make. As Moses told Joshua in Deuteronomy 31:8: "The LORD is the one who is marching before you! He is the one who will be with you! He won't let you down. He won't abandon you. So don't be afraid or scared!"

*There will always be the gawkers, the disgusted, and the too-afraid-to-ask. It is their choice, and their loss, to stay that way.*

The fight for independence is grueling, confusing, and never-ending when one's body won't cooperate. I will always have to work against our culture's stereotypes along with my own bias and ignorance. It will always be a struggle for me to know how to balance my need for autonomy with others' God-given desire to help. But what comfort I have when I know that I serve a God who doesn't waste a tear I shed. Every heartache will see redemption. In every hurt I have the choice to look for

God's presence . . . God is with me in it. He creates life from nothingness, and His love changes everything it touches. Isaiah 43:19 says, "Look! I'm doing a new thing; now it sprouts up; don't you recognize it? I'm making a way in the desert, paths in the wilderness." But sometimes God's love reaches us in the most unexpected ways. Rivers of life can spring up at the most unexpected times.

What comfort I have when I know that I serve a God who doesn't waste a tear I shed.

CHAPTER 7

# JUST PEOPLE
# FALLING IN LOVE

When I checked my messages that day on MySpace, there was one from someone I'd never met. The fact that he'd sent the message wasn't the strange part—it was the content. He was asking me on a date. A for-real, let's-meet-for-dinner type of date, and I'd never seen him in person in my life. It's been almost seven years since he sent that message, and since that time it's become much more common for people to find their "match" online, but in 2006 it was still a little sketchy and the thought didn't particularly appeal to me. I'd seen too many TV specials featuring Internet stalkers.

Standing in the college's newsroom, I laughed to my friend Lindsay, "Some guy on MySpace just asked me on a date. Like, a *date* date."

"Who is it?" she asked, wanting more details.

"I don't know, his screen name is 'adamkvc.'"

"Hmm . . . Adam Kovac! Is it Adam Kovac?"

"All I know is 'adamkvc'. . . maybe."

I pulled up his profile and Lindsay knew him immediately. "I went to high school with him! He's a really nice guy," she said. "You should give him a chance!"

I figured a nice guy might be a welcome change of pace, so I agreed to meet him at the Dairy Queen down the street. I chose that location because it was a well-lit, open area and hey, I've never heard of anyone being abducted from our Dairy Queen. After I told him I'd take him up on the date, however, I began to worry that he hadn't noticed my disability from my pictures. There were several I'd posted that showed my arms, but people frequently don't see that I'm different until I start *doing* something different.

I opened a chat window, and cringed as I started typing. I told him "I don't know if you realized this, but I was born with a birth defect that made my arms small and weak, so I have to do everything with my feet. I would totally understand if you wanted to skip the date. I just wanted to make sure you knew."

I sat and waited for a reply. I imagined he was probably going back through my pictures to see what he had previously missed. I thought he probably wished he had seen it *before* he'd asked me on the date. Now, he looks like a jerk if he cancels. I guessed he would take me on one date and that would be the end of that. He finally replied that he did not want to cancel our ice cream date.

Recently, I asked Adam what he was really thinking when I told him about my disability, expecting to hear an honest reply of frustration or dismay. "I was shocked that I hadn't noticed the disability and had to be told," he said. "I thought, maybe I was temporarily blinded, which means we were meant to meet. I never felt any emotion that was negative or depressing. All I felt and cared about was this very attractive girl is here talking to me and I was even more anxious to ask her out and meet her."

When the time came for me to leave for Dairy Queen, I thought about making up some excuse to cancel and even got online and told Adam that I was all gross from packing and moving all day (thereby giving him an out if he didn't really want to do this). I was absolutely con-vinced that once he saw me as I am, doing the things I do, he would regret asking me out, and there would cer-tainly be no second date. I imagined that if I was ever to find love, surely it would be with someone who knew me as a friend first. Someone who appreciated who I was on the *inside* enough to tolerate the outside. This "I think you're cute, let's go out" scenario was doomed to fail.

He didn't take my easy out and told me one didn't need to be dressed up to go to Dairy Queen, so there was no can-celing. I hopped in the car, drove the couple minutes, and pulled into the parking lot where a person who looked like Adam was leaning on the building, talking on the phone. I tried to park my car perfectly. I stepped out, and he hung up and smiled. This was happening. We ordered our ice cream and sat down. I don't remember a thing we talked about or even how long we were there. But I remember his smile. I remember that he didn't flinch or gawk or even ask questions when I started eating with my feet. I remember the moment I realized he was laughing so much because he was . . . *nervous?* He was nervous? Even after seeing how I was, *what* I was, he still liked me enough to care if he impressed me or not. Incredible. It seemed too good to be true. I remained skeptical.

If you ask Adam about that first date now, he will respond,

I was nervous not because I was meeting someone with a disability but because I was just meeting someone. First impressions are always important. I assume my feelings were just like anyone else who meets Sarah for the first time. Except, my strategy for first impressions was a priority. I was 100 percent focused on her eyes, questions, and responses. I wasn't going to make it obvious that I was amazed by her talent. Yes, my thoughts were probably like anyone else's. You want to stare with amazement, curiosity, and ask a million questions. But I didn't. Time would answer all the questions for me if she was willing to give me a chance. To do that, my first impression was important and so that was my focus.

We finished our ice cream and went our separate ways. I was surprised that a man would ever be drawn to my looks and not repulsed when he saw the full picture. I was surprised that he didn't seem to be a man with a short-term agenda, like I had attracted many times before. But I was most surprised when, a couple of days later, he called and asked me on another date. After all, I am no man's idea of perfect. I highly doubt any man fantasizes about the one he loves being gawked at or treated rudely while they're out to eat. Who would want all the emotional work that comes with loving someone like me? I had doubts that such a man even existed, and once this one figured out what he was dealing with, he'd realize his mistake.

We went on a few more dates and had a couple of movie nights at his house and all the while I was bracing myself for the inevitable. Time would start to lengthen between these invitations, and eventually we would settle into that comfortable "friend" zone. We would speak kindly of each other and I would say we used to be together, but he probably wouldn't talk about it. I thought he must have a very tender heart for dragging it out this long (or maybe a cruel one). Surely he just didn't want me to know he didn't like me in "that way" because of my differences. But it was OK—I would survive it.

One evening, however, as I said good-bye and had turned to walk out the door, he wheeled me around and kissed me right on the lips. It was actually quite romantic, but I was so shocked I think I ruined the moment. I just stiffened, and when he let me go, I pretty much just said, "OK, good night!" and bolted. I was stunned. That was no move to make if he just wanted to be my friend. Was it possible that I could end up with the classic love story? He sees her, he is attracted, he pursues her, they fall in love. I never thought this was something I could have, but here it was unfolding before me. Surely he'd been around me enough to recognize the baggage I brought to the relationship, and there was no shortage of others willing to point that fact out to him. But whether it made sense or not, he wanted to be with me. And it didn't take long before I started to realize that my future looked incomplete without him.

Adam says now:

> Relationships are relationships, they're never easy and sacrifice and compromise must be made by both partners for a happy relationship to work. I knew this before I met Sarah and was prepared from the start. I did wonder about some of the physical things. Holding hands wasn't hard. I did wonder the first time if she would be nervous or embarrassed when I grabbed hold of her hand, but there were no complaints so I guess it was OK. I wondered how we would hug. I wondered if I would get back and foot rubs and massages. Turns out none of that is a problem. I couldn't be happier.

I'd love to be able to say that Adam and I had a slow and deliberate courtship, but we didn't. We both had waited for what seemed like so long to find each other and now that we had, we didn't want to spend a moment apart. We did not take our time to savor the dating process, and I wish we hadn't shortchanged ourselves in that way. But we saw where the relationship was headed and felt no need to waste any time getting there. We were inseparable, almost from the moment we met.

One of our first dates was an outing to a mall about thirty minutes away. I had gotten all dolled-up at my dorm before he picked me up in his little green Malibu for the drive. We exchanged nervous small talk all the way there, and I kept my feet on the floorboard, and in their shoes. (I would usually sit cross-legged and be using my feet to fiddle with my hair and makeup.) I still wasn't sure if he was ready for me to be *me* 100 percent of the time.

We arrived, walked through the doors, and he grabbed my hand. Tears welled up in my eyes. Nobody had ever held my hand in that way. If someone had to hold my hand, it was forever an awkward ordeal, as no one knew how. My fingers being so small and curved don't fit nicely into the average palm. But Adam just went for it. He didn't want to hide me like some others had. I felt like I was being paraded through the mall that day. For the first time, I felt like I was worth parading.

Not quite a year after Adam and I started dating, he accompanied my family on a vacation to the Colorado Rockies. It is tradition that we rent a hidden-away cabin for a week and do very little but fish, play games, hike around, and sleep . . . but sleep is the only truly mandatory activity. I knew that Adam wanted to propose to me sometime in the near future, but I'd told him that it would make me happy if he would speak to my dad about it first. This vacation would be the perfect time! The relaxing view, the peace and quiet . . . my dad is never happier than when he's fly fishing a Colorado stream. I suggested to Adam that, if he was going to do it, this vacation might be the easiest time.

All throughout the week, I found quiet moments to anxiously ask Adam if it had *happened* yet. Did he talk to Dad while they were fishing the lake? over breakfast? while I was doing my hair? No, no, and no. I wondered if

Adam even wanted to talk to my dad since he didn't seem to be trying very hard. The week passed and Adam never got his sit-down with his potential father-in-law. I was disappointed and confused. It would come to light at a much later date that my father had guessed Adam was planning to ask about marrying me, and he'd been hiding. He wasn't ready to give away his little girl, so he avoided Adam like the plague. If they ended up alone together, Dad would suddenly have some urgent thing to do, and thus Adam chased my father all over the mountain for a whole week without getting his conversation. It's actually pretty impressive that my dad managed to pull this off considering the whole vacation was arranged around the idea of having *nothing* to do! But this was his only child, his little girl. A dad has to run away sometimes.

*We want unconditional love. Peace. Beauty. Family. To be part of something big. We have so much in common.*

A few weeks later, Adam was determined to get it done. He set a time to meet my dad at their house to talk. He left for their meeting and hours passed as I wondered what they might be discussing and prayed it was going well. Adam brought back the report that it would be a little longer before he could propose with my father's blessing, but after some more months passed, we would most certainly be engaged. Imagine my surprise when a couple of weeks later he showed up at my door with a bouquet of roses and a card. I can't remember the details of the event or the words of the card. But I remember that he wrote how much he loved me, how happy I made him, and when I looked up, I remember my heart nearly leapt from my chest. He was down on one knee. He pulled one rose from the bunch—it was fake and I hadn't even noticed. The bud opened on a hinge and inside was a beautiful, princess-cut diamond engagement ring. I said yes with tears in my eyes, slipped it on my size 1 ring finger, and we went straight to tell my parents (who had given Adam the go-ahead weeks ago when they met . . . he had me fooled). We were going to be married! I couldn't believe it was happening.

❖ ❖ ❖

When Adam proposed that June afternoon, the wedding venue was the furthest thing from my mind. Later, as we needed to start making plans, we decided to marry at the Catholic church Adam's family attended. But as we began premarital counseling there, we learned that we could not be wed in that church unless we planned to raise our children in the Catholic tradition. Since we instead wanted to raise any children at my home church, we decided to find another venue. It was then that I remembered that not long before meeting Adam, I had watched my best friend plan a wedding. I knew all those details would just overwhelm me if it were *my* wedding, and I would be completely miserable instead of enjoying the experience. So I pitched the idea of a destination wedding to Adam. We were in agreement except that he wanted a cruise and I wanted a resort. The "destination" for our destination wedding was ultimately decided by a coin toss. (He didn't yet know that I am one of the luckiest people alive.)

We booked a trip to a resort in Punta Cana, Dominican Republic, for a ten-day stay, including a wedding on the beach, a horse-drawn carriage for my arrival, a phenomenal photographer, and a wedding coordinator. I didn't have to do a thing but show up, get pampered, and say "I do." Definitely a detail-phobe's dream come true! My mom, however, could not resist planning a reception when we returned home with much help from our dear friend Charla. So, in the end we had a dream wedding and were able to share our happiness with our friends and family too.

✦ ✦ ✦

Like every newlywed couple, our first year was spent learning, adjusting, and beginning to see ourselves as one. At times, our new life together was a difficult transition. On top of first-year frustrations, there was the small matter of my fiercely independent nature versus Adam's desire to help me, his new bride.

A certain afternoon comes to mind when I think of this topic. I was cooking spaghetti (one of the very few things I could cook at the time), and I had sat on the floor to open the jar of sauce. Let me help you get that mental picture. In order for me to open a jar, I first lay it on its side on the ground. I put my left foot on the bottom of the jar to steady it, and then I use my right foot and hand simultaneously to push/pull the lid, thereby twisting it. I turn it just enough to pop the seal, set the jar upright, and open it the rest of the way very easily using just my feet.

Adam walked in the kitchen and saw me sitting on the floor, with a jar of bright red spaghetti sauce on its side. I was yanking at the lid, and he went into a bit of a panic, no doubt envisioning our dinner spilled all over the linoleum.

"Here, let me do that!" he lurched toward me.

"I've got it." I turned away to stop him from taking the jar. This was a particularly stubborn jar, and I'd been wrestling with it for a few minutes. I wanted to conquer it.

"You're going to spill it!" Adam stepped closer and I could feel every muscle in my body tense up. "I've done this before, Adam! Do you know how many times I've made spaghetti? All I ever cook is pasta!" If I were an animal I would have snarled. Instead, we just escalated quickly into a lengthy yelling match about how I was being stubborn, and he was being disrespectful.

That wouldn't be the last argument we'd have over my need for independence and his need to help. Luckily, my parents got me an electric jar opener for Christmas, so spaghetti sauce would no longer be a point of friction in our marriage.

It took me some time to realize that my husband is not the "them" in the me-versus-them life I was used to. I'd spent so much time trying to prove myself, trying to earn respect, clawing for independence, I didn't know what to do now that it was no longer just me. How was I to maintain my independence now that I was part of a team? Gradually, I learned to relax a little, to let go of my need to prove myself to him. And gradually, he came to understand that sometimes there are things I have to prove to myself, even if it would be easier and faster (and less messy?) for him to just do them for me.

*I saw that the achievements I'd clung to were blinding me to the value I have, simply because I've been created.*

Sometimes I *need* to struggle. And sometimes, the best way he can help me is to just know that struggle and I are old friends. We rarely need intervention.

As I write this, Adam and I have been married just over four years. From the very beginning, we couldn't have been more different. Even beyond the denominational differences we faced, he likes country western music, I like smooth jazz. He likes meat and potatoes, I eat meat only occasionally. He likes physically challenging activities (dirt biking, snowboarding), I like to work out my mind (reading, discussing). We were very literally from opposite ends of town and had virtually nothing in common. But from the first moment we spent together, his presence was warmth. At first, I felt a bit deflated because he didn't appreciate some of the talents people had been praising me for my whole life. He wasn't blown away by my art or trumpet playing or poetry. I was disappointed that he didn't seem to appreciate the creative side of me. But I started to realize that, as much as Adam loved me, he couldn't fill *every* relational need I have in my life. He and I are not in a vacuum, we need other friends too. But the one thing he has always given me that no one else can is a sense of validation.

As we grew to know each other better, I started to appreciate how difficult it can be to impress him with the creativity I've always allowed to define me. After a few times having my work passed back to me accompanied by nothing but a shrug and an "it's nice," I realized that there are indeed people who see the world differently. There are people who think differently from my parents and do not automatically believe something is brilliant just because I made it. I realized that good art should be able to touch anybody, regardless of background, previous exposure, or education. Art can bypass the mind and hold the very heart of a person. That was the kind of writing, speaking, art I decided I wanted to begin to create. What good is it if I can move someone who already thinks like me? I began to look for what we all have in common.

In art and in life, we have the choice to look for either those things that divide us or those that bring us together. We can argue the finer points of theology and politics, pick apart each other's ways of living, and criticize the unfamiliar, but there are common threads that bind us all together. We all long for love, acceptance, respect, beauty, peace. We all want to feel part of something larger than ourselves—that foot-of-the-mountain,

*Journal:* Who are those people in your life that you have nothing in common with? Dig deeper. Is it really true you have nothing in common? What are the things that could provide common ground to share and develop?

edge-of-the-ocean knowledge that we could never see it all, experience it all, learn it all is the adventure every human knows well. We want a home, a place to belong. A place of quiet spirit. A place our souls can be healed. A place where self is enough and love is not something to be worked for, only to be accepted. To be immersed in, to be given without any thought of repayment. We want unconditional love. Peace. Beauty. Family. To be part of something big. We have so much in common.

When I met Adam, I expected him to fall in love with the things about me that made me unique: my quirky sense of humor, my passion for the arts, the way I thought. But it turned out that he loved the things about me that will never change. He loved the things that tie us to- gether, the things that make me just a person. We were just people falling in love. Sometimes he is enthusiastic about my writing, often he now likes my art, but always he loves the person I am underneath all that, after the pretenses of education and culture are stripped away. Our relationship forced me to ask myself what I had to

*Journal:* What are the achievements, success, and talents that you have told yourself "make you you"?

Is that all you are? Who is the you behind those achievements?

Who are the people in your life who recognize the real you?

offer without my talent and education. At first I didn't believe there was anything else. But as I began to see myself through the eyes of this man, I saw that the achievements I'd clung to were blinding me to the value I have, simply because I've been created. Because God breathed life into me, because I, not my talents, am a child of God. I am special not because I'm different, but because I'm the same.

It may sound funny, but Adam made me feel so . . . average. So commonplace. I was not someone unique to be gawked at or someone "other" who was below him. I just *was* whatever I wanted to be. It was refreshing. It was romantic. It was liberating. And as we started our life together, I learned to laugh and relax and *be* in a way I had never been with someone other than my immediate family. He was my family now, and I knew I'd chosen well. The road ahead would not be easy, but this was the kind of man I wanted to walk that road with. A man who would hold my hand proudly and let people stare, because he knows who and what I am, even when others don't.

CHAPTER 8

# LOSING IT ALL

I had everything I wanted: a great husband, a nice house, a dog, and two cats. I was enjoying college and being a newlywed. I felt like I finally, *finally*, had caught up with my peers. I had the life of a typical American twenty-something. I felt accomplished arriving at that place. In fact, I think I could have died a happy woman at the age of twenty-four. I had worked as an adult to acquire the skills of putting on a necklace using my feet and teeth, getting a boiling pot of pasta from the stove to the sink to strain, typing thirty-five words per minute with my toes, tying the string in drawstring pants, and cutting up my own steak. My adult life was already incredibly fulfilling when I thought of all the things I'd worked for, all the things I'd won in a few short years.

For someone with a disability, autonomy is sort of the holy grail of life goals, and I was darn close. I could taste it. There was rarely a situation that presented itself that I wasn't ready to handle. For the first time, I felt like I was in control of my life. There wasn't something just out of my reach that I felt the need to claw and fight for. I was known to go around on sunny days singing the chorus from a Crosby, Stills, Nash, and Young song: "Life used to be so hard, / now everything is easy, 'cause of you." True, validating, empowering love had completely changed my life, even in such a short time. I was no longer the sulking, bitter girl I'd been. I was a different person. But love wasn't done with me yet.

❖ ❖ ❖

We had been married for nearly a year, and the discussion of children came up. I was in no hurry to have kids and had no problem saying so. I'd always felt really awkward around them, never knowing quite how to respond to their pointing and staring, never knowing how to hold or care for them. Besides, I hadn't yet graduated college.

If and when I did have children, I always thought I'd like to keep it at one. I was an only child and loved being so close with my parents. They were my best friends. I didn't wish for siblings and was happy with the arrangement. I thought it would be nice to really focus my love and attention on the one child instead of

*To identify the seed God has entrusted us with is only the beginning of our work. We have a lifetime of weeding, watering, and nourishing ahead of us.*

having a whole gaggle running me ragged. My house growing up was pretty quiet and peaceful. It seemed to me the more people you have living in a place, the more difficult it will be to maintain that blissful peace.

However, Adam, coming from a large family, felt that he was way behind in the procreation game. He was twenty-seven and had none of the thirty-two children he'd planned on having by this time. I exaggerate, but he really did want to move the process along. He loved children, and every time we saw one, he'd elbow and mention how cute the baby was and that he'd be more than happy to provide me with one.

After much persuading on his part, and heel-digging on mine, I no more than *thought* the word "maybe" before we found out I was expecting. I looked at the pregnancy test in shock for a moment before I carried it down to show Adam, who I assumed would do backflips of joy. I showed him the results and all he said was, "Are you serious?" I can't remember if I became angry, cried, or both, but I was not happy with his lack of enthusiasm considering I was the one who had been uncertain and he had been the one wanting to hurry things along. But after the initial shock wore off in the following minutes, we both started to anticipate the new life ahead and wondered how we'd tell the rest of the family. I went to my mother at her office first. I was afraid my parents might be disappointed in the timing since I hadn't finished college, or they might be concerned that I hadn't thought this through. When I told her, she was completely speechless. Like, no words. This was a great start. My anxiety must have been obvious when I went to tell my dad, because he responded with confusion, "Is this good news?" I replied that of course it was. So, of course they were happy.

After initially breaking the news, I was so excited to make grandparents of both sets of our parents for the very first time. I felt I was creating and bringing forth from myself the ultimate gift for these people whom I held so dear. I felt such joy that I could do something to bring so much happiness. It brought me to tears on more than one occasion. Granted, when I was pregnant most things brought me to tears, but still . . .

We've never liked secrets and had no desire to keep our big news quiet, so soon we announced it on Facebook and to the world. There was no shortage of encouragement, support, and joy in the responses I received, but along with a wave of positive energy

*You never want to pray for God to make you a gracious person because God might just do what's necessary to make that happen.*

came comments here and there that made me question whether I was ready for this. I know no one is ever really *ready* to be a parent; we grow into the role. However, when someone asks you how you'll carry your child, how you'll transport your child, what you'll do if your child starts choking, and you have no answer—well, I started to question myself in ways I never had before.

It frustrated me that people I'd never met were sending messages asking how I'd do this or that. I even had a couple people flat-out tell me what I wouldn't be able to do. "Well," they patronized, "Adam will just have to do all the things you can't manage." This stuff probably shouldn't bother me after nearly thirty years of dealing with it, but it never stops hurting. Every false assumption is a fresh reminder that I am not seen as capable of dealing with my own life. Despite the fact that I have learned to play the trumpet, drive a car without modifications, had a job, lived alone, and attended college, I will never accomplish enough to be seen as an equal by the general public. People will always make snap judgments before getting to know me.

When I was pregnant with Ethan, the most difficult part of being questioned like this was that I couldn't snap back with an answer. I'd never dealt with babies. I'd changed one diaper in my life. I had never spent time alone with an infant and no, I had no idea how I'd get him in and out of a crib, how I'd carry him, how I'd get him into a car seat, or what bath time was going to look like.

I was not trying to look into the future and logic my way through bathing a wet, squirming baby. I had never held a squirming baby—even a dry one. I had no reference point to allow me to reason my way to a solution to these issues. So when asked how I might handle a certain situation, all I could do was say, "I don't know yet." As badly as I wanted answers to spit back in people's faces, as

*Journal:* What did you want to be when you grew up? More importantly, who did you want to be?

badly as I wanted to make them feel sorry they questioned me, it was a humbling period in my life.

I knew the answers would come, but for the time, I had to try my best to be hurt without hurting back, to remember that people weren't making these assumptions or asking these questions to hurt me, and if they knew how it felt, they probably wouldn't.

When I was a little girl, I remember overhearing my parents and some of their friends having a conversation about grace. They were joking that you never want to pray for God to make you a gracious person because he might just do what's necessary to make that happen. I thought and thought about what they were saying. I understood

*When we change, it means we are allowing space for ourselves to become something more than we thought we were.*

that God had to let you go through some difficult things, painful things, if you were going to learn grace, but I wanted it. So I prayed, so sincerely, that God would turn me into a woman of grace, who would respond to others with grace even when they weren't being gracious to me. I knew that God heard me and would honor my request.

I believe it's no coincidence that that memory still comes to the forefront of my thoughts so often. I see that little girl and the woman she wants to grow to be. And now I am presented constantly with opportunities to learn and practice grace. To be generous in my assumptions about others and kind when others aren't. Some days I can handle anything thrown at me, and some days it would be best if I just avoided all people. But lucky for me, God doesn't have "off" days. God is gracious even in my disgrace. And forgiveness waits ready the moment I judge, when my words snarl, when I lose focus of who I'm meant to be. There is forgiveness. There is another chance with every new encounter. Every imperfect person in my life is my second, third, trillionth shot at becoming the Sarah I begged God to make me twenty years ago. Or, perhaps that woman was already in me as a child. Maybe my desire to be gracious was evidence of the

*Journal:* Far more important than any vocation you could dream up, there is a person you were designed to be. Maybe you didn't see hints of in your childhood, but I bet you can now, if you try. Do you ever wish you could find more ways, time, means to help the poor? Encourage with your words instead of gossiping? Be more thankful? Connect with nature? Disconnect from technology? Create peace in your relationships? Spend time in quiet or with groups? Be more self-controlled? These desires might just be hinting at what God has in mind for you.

presence of grace itself, begging not to be buried by life, sin, worries, pride, growing up.

I return often to James 1:5: "Anyone who needs wisdom should ask God, whose very nature is to give to everyone without a second thought, without keeping score. Wisdom will certainly be given to those who ask." Whenever I've heard this verse I've often wondered why God so easily guarantees the gift of wisdom. Maybe because only the wise would ask for it in the first place, so they're asking for something they've already been granted. Maybe, just maybe, our Creator, the Master Gardener, already planted in us the seeds to be the person he intended us to be. Galatians 1:15 tells us: "God had set me apart from birth and called me through his grace."

Before you were born, God had a plan for you, and maybe there have been hints here and there indicating what that plan might be. Sometimes children have an uncomplicated view of things that makes it easier to identify what lies buried deep in the soul. Maybe, like me, you had a strong drive to help animals or preserve nature. Maybe compassion and empathy were natural for you. Maybe you loved giving gifts to others or helping strangers. Maybe you had ideas about what kind of woman or man you'd like to grow up to be. Yes, I had my dreams of becoming an astronaut or the first woman president. But deeper than that, God placed in each of us unique character strengths that make us irreplaceable assets to our community.

There are so many types of people, so many needed parts of this community God has created. We each have an important contribution to *I can't fail so big that* make by simply being the person *God won't catch me.* God created us to be. It's simple, but it's certainly isn't easy, is it? To identify the seed God has entrusted us with is only the beginning of our work. We have a lifetime of weeding, watering, and nourishing ahead of us. Every time I react to someone out of irritation, I have to remember what I'm trying to grow, what God wants to grow in me. I have to let my little seedling of grace out into the sun, or it will forever be overshadowed by a jungle of pride, bitterness, and anger that I've chosen to cultivate instead. I don't have to make myself into the person I want to be—I only have to choose which bits of my being I'm going to feed and which I'm going to let die.

I was confident that God had already given me strengths needed to work through all the new challenges of being a mother. Many times previously in life, I'd found myself dealing with situations that had no clear solution, and it came naturally to me to stay calm and work through to an answer. For example, I didn't know how I would drive a car until the day my dad took me out one morning to teach me in our church parking lot. I thought my arms might be strong enough to steer, Dad thought it made the most sense for me to use my left leg, but I ended up settling on my right leg for steering and the left for the gas and brake pedals. The day before I learned to drive, you could have asked me how I would do it, and I wouldn't have had a clear answer for you—but I wasn't worried. There was no doubt in my mind that I would find my way. It would become clear when I was sitting in the driver's seat.

I knew it would be the same with this baby. Once I was in the moment, when I *had* to carry him from one place to another, God would give me a creative and safe idea. I was, after all, his mother. No one could be more concerned for his safety than I would be. I thought that everyone else would naturally have this same confidence in my ability to adapt—after watching all the things I've found my way around and through over the years, how could anyone doubt that I could keep a baby safe?

A couple months into the pregnancy my dad had an idea: "Why don't you try working with one of those life-sized baby dolls they use in high schools to help students learn about responsibility?" he asked. He thought maybe I could practice holding it, since they are the size and weight of a real baby. Under normal—nonpregnant—

circumstances, such an idea might sting a little, but I would have been able to concede that it made sense. Offer that same advice to a hormoned-out, sleep-deprived *pregnant* me, and all I heard was, "I, your father, don't trust you to adapt on your own. You're going to kill my grandchild." A fit of shrieking and wailing ensued, as anyone who's ever been pregnant or lived with a pregnant woman might imagine. Of course, my dad's motives were good, and what he said made some sense. But because too often in my life, responsibilities have been snatched from me without my permission by strangers who thought they knew what I could handle and what I couldn't, this felt like that same scenario. I *knew* I could adjust to this baby when it came and felt that worrying about the "how" too much beforehand was not only a waste of emotional energy, but more than likely a waste of time—not to mention demeaning.

Truthfully, I didn't know what I was getting into. Does anyone? Becoming a parent is challenging for the most physically capable among us. Some obstacles would be more difficult to overcome than others; some obstacles

*Journal:* Have you ever failed "so big" that you feel God shouldn't/won't help you out? Do you sometimes feel there's a limit to God's grace and mercy in your life?

would overcome me. But the most crippling issues I would face had little to do with my arms. I would need to find the strength, beg God for the grace, to trust myself even when others didn't. I would need to trust that I can't fail so big that God won't catch me.

As the months wore on, I tried to keep my calm as my stomach grew ever bigger. It was a particularly hot Missouri summer, and I figured I'd probably not be spending much time at the pool for the rest of my life, so I didn't want to waste the perfect swimming weather. I can only imagine what people thought when this eight-month pregnant woman showed up in a two-piece swimsuit at the city's water park, waddled up to the front counter and swiped my debit card with my foot like it was nothing. I thought this was my last opportunity to wear two-piece swimwear, so heck if I was letting a few stares stop me from enjoying the sunshine. It became more difficult to use my feet for things as the pregnancy progressed; getting your feet up to your face to eat is hard enough without a watermelon for a belly. But what was I going to do—not eat? So up until the night Ethan was born, I was eating, driving, brushing my teeth, and so on with my feet to my face, but I was completely exhausted. If I attempted to drive for more than five minutes, I experienced shooting pains down my back and leg. I could only lean forward and eat one or two bites before I had to lean back and return my leg to the floor. The baby was starting to crowd my spine, and every one of these activities require a lot of abdominal work. My abs were shoving the baby into my already-tender middle back, and daily tasks were almost unbearable.

I would not go so far as to ask for help eating (though Adam did offer, bless his heart), but my mom spent a fair amount of time chauffeuring me to and from my prenatal checkups. Of course I'd chosen a hospital forty-five minutes away instead of the one five minutes down the road.

It was sobering, watching the independence I'd worked so hard for slip away over the course of a few short months. Would it ever come back, or would I just be relying on others in new ways once the baby came? I feared that this was the beginning of the end of everything I wanted. Everything I thought I'd won. All I ever worked for, independence and the respect to be gained with it for someone in my position, was in the past. Who would I be without my disdain for help?

*Journal:* Where in your life will you dare to ask yourself these questions: "Can I be more?" "Can I do better?" "Is this the best I have to give?" Explore what being more, doing better, giving your best looks like in each situation you want to address.

I began to have this dark premonition that my life was about to irreversibly change in every way. I was afraid I was about to lose everything important. In reality, my idea of what was important was about to be turned on its head.

Change is hard. And scary. Change requires of us more than we think we can give. When we change, it means we are allowing space for ourselves to become something more than we think we are. How easy it is to box ourselves in, label ourselves, and never force ourselves to ask the questions, "Can I be more?" "Can I do better?" "Is this the best I have to give?"

❖ ❖ ❖

Were you ever privileged to be exposed to Aesop's fables as a child? A lesser-known story comes to mind, called "The Fox and the Grapes."

> A famished fox saw some clusters of ripe grapes hanging from a trellised vine. She resorted to all her tricks to get at them, but wearied herself in vain, for she could not reach them. At last she turned away, hiding her disappointment and saying: "The Grapes are sour, and not ripe as I thought." (*Æesop's Fables* [London/New York: George Routledge and Sons, 1918], 34)

For much of my young life, I claimed I didn't ever want to have children. They never seemed to like me much, and dirty diapers held no appeal for me. At least, these were some of my excuses for shying away from the idea. Without even jumping for the grapes, I had decided they were out of my reach—sour grapes. It wasn't a conscious decision, but I'd seen how nervous people got when I wanted to hold babies. I'd watched children run away from me and call me a monster. The time I was in Barcelona, Spain, with my youth group, I was swarmed by children shouting at me in Spanish. I knew enough Spanish to know they were asking what was wrong with my hands, but I didn't speak well enough to answer them. I just stood, paralyzed, humiliated in this sea of children who weren't getting the hint that they were making me uncomfortable and I didn't have the facility to answer them. They shouted louder and louder (now I know what it feels like when we talk louder to immigrants, thinking that will help), until finally our translator came and said something I didn't understand to usher them elsewhere.

*Journal:* In what situations do you feel unprepared for the job or task at hand? Do you feel you don't have what it takes to be the spouse/parent/coworker you need to be? What are your biggest challenges in preparing—heart, mind, and spirit—for the job?

Any relationship I'd had with a child was always tainted by their distancing questions. "Why is she like that?" "What's wrong with her?" The questions were usually whispered to the child's mom or saved for later, but sometimes asked of me, to the parent's embarrassment. Before I go on, I realize that children seeing someone different and asking questions is a good thing. A *great* thing. They need to be exposed to all kinds of people and knowledge, or else they will grow up in a very small, shallow world. But to be the one on the other end of those questions, and asking myself if I was "Mom" material, added to the unease.

I doubted that any child would ever feel safe, at home in my arms, when they all obviously could see I wasn't the same. What child would want *these* arms above all others? How could a person as broken as me ever find the strength to support someone else? Impossible.

I closed my mind to the idea. I hardened my heart to the need. I didn't need anybody, in fact. I rejected children before they ever had the chance to reject me . . . heartache averted.

But then, love.

Someone loved me, trusted me enough to tie his future to mine. Believed in me enough to want to lay his children in these fragile arms. He believed that I had what it took to be a *great* mom, just as I was. Sometimes I dared to believe him. Sometimes I could believe that all it took to be a nurturer was already in me, just waiting to bloom. Sometimes I trusted that God would not abandon me to failure in life.

And sometimes I was terrified and felt completely unprepared and asked God if we'd made a terrible mistake. Sometimes Adam and I would argue about something ridiculous and I would wonder how we would hold it together with a baby in the mix. Sometimes I wondered what in the world made me think I could care for a baby as my most basic skills nearly slipped away during pregnancy. But the baby was coming. Whether I was going to succeed or fail at this "mom" thing, it was coming. All Adam and I could do now was hold hands and hold on, because we had no idea how this was going to work.

*Journal:* Have you ever been able not to "be anxious"—not to worry—about anything like the letter to the Philippians says?

What are some beginning places for you?

A way of prayer, a passing over of the burden

to God that allows you to give over your worry?

# CHAPTER 9

# IN CAPABLE ARMS

The world was about to change, and I was the only one who felt the full weight of it. The rolling, kicking, pressing weight of it was with me all day and kept me up all night. Would Adam and I be good parents? Would everyone else be happy? I felt so unprepared. So incapable.

Little did I know that my heart would be transformed

in a million tiny ways. I was about to embark on a journey of trust. I would learn that while I couldn't trust others to always be the encouragement I needed, and I
certainly couldn't trust myself or Adam to be perfect,
there is One who is perfect. There is One who *never* fails.
God is ever-present, with words that are truth. And His
arms are strong, capable, and ready to help. God knew
what the future held, and wasn't worried. He knew my
every shortcoming . . . and God wasn't worried. Think
about that. The only one with all the information, who
knows all the secrets, sees all our failures and fears, says to
us through Paul, "Don't be anxious about anything;
rather, bring up all of your requests to God in your prayers
and petitions, along with giving thanks" (Philippians
4:6). God says, "Relax. I've got this." The trick is, of
course, letting God have it . . . letting God have us. It's
so easy to instead believe the louder voices telling us we
have to perform . . . we have to be enough . . . we have to
stay in control.

It seemed like any control I'd had over the goings-on of
my own life had been ripped from me during my last few
months of pregnancy. All that was left to me, really, was
planning for the baby's arrival. But I couldn't even help
with the remodeling of the nursery or do much "nesting."
So I just read and planned and read some more until I had
some very firm ideas about how exactly I wanted this

baby to enter the world. People looked at me like I was nuts for wanting a natural childbirth and for wanting to use cloth diapers afterward. I am not sure why this surprised anyone, since I rarely do things the conventional way. I was so blessed to have my mother's encouragement on this and many other aspects of parenting that had the potential to go wrong. I don't know how she felt through the whole pregnancy, but she made *me* feel that my wishes were totally reasonable and that I would certainly succeed.

*Joy, even joy so intense, rarely comes without struggle.*

My husband took a little warming up to the lengthy drive to my open-minded OB-GYN's office and the hospital with which she was affiliated. Actually, all the way up to the birth I'm pretty sure he was just trying to grin and bear my newfound hippie tendencies. In hindsight, though, he's said (unsolicited) that next time around, he would want it to happen the same way.

I believe it was because my abs stayed so active (from using my feet to eat, bathe, drive, and so on) throughout the pregnancy that the contractions didn't feel quite as intense as I was told they would. I didn't feel anything contracting at all and wasn't even sure I was in labor until just before my water broke.

I had stayed up late that night, and Adam was soon to

leave for his shift at work when I realized something might be happening. I thought my contractions were about seven minutes apart, so I woke Adam up and hopped in the shower, because I wanted to have fresh makeup and hair for the "new mommy" pictures. (Right.) I was in the shower just long enough to get my hair wet and drip the day's makeup all down my face, when the contractions became so strong that I couldn't stand. So much for the postbirth Glamour Shot.

*Think about this: the only One with all the information, who knows all the secrets, sees all our failures and fears, says . . . "Relax. I've got this."*

Adam found something big and comfortable for me to wear to the hospital. The contractions were three minutes apart now, and I was in so much pain that I didn't even care that he picked out probably the most embarrassing outfit possible: my snarkiest maternity shirt (a garage sale purchase with an arrow pointing to my belly with the words "THIS is my attitude problem!" and some questionable Rolling Stones boxer shorts, which I'd carried over from my college days. Come to think of it, I may well have looked like a long-lost member of an eighties hair band, considering my makeup had smeared all over my face in the shower and my perm was now air drying.

My mother had given me a book to read a couple months before. It was called *Supernatural Childbirth*. This book contained, among other things, a few women's testimonies of trusting God to have pain-free birthing experiences, and it was an encouragement to other women of faith that they could have the same experience. I don't like to think I am a cynical person—maybe *realist* is a better word. I read this book and thought, *That sounds lovely, but I don't think I have that kind of faith*. I had mentally prepared myself for pain, and I was at peace with the idea. I thought, *I have endured excruciating pain before. I can do it again.* I read numerous books on childbirth and many natural birth stories, and I knew I could push through the pain like a champ. But, when I was riding for what seemed an eternity in my parents' Tahoe on the way to the hospital, my contractions at their peak intensity, every bump in the road jackhammering my pelvis, all I could think was, *"Oh Lord, I have FAITH! I believe!"* Maybe the Lord deemed my last-minute-labor faith as too little, too late.

Funny how just the thought of pain can be such a scary thing. Even if we know something good is waiting on the other side, it's hard to see anything but the difficulty before us. Jesus has been there: in the garden of Gethsemane the Savior of the World asked the Father if it might be possible to find another way. He was feeling no lashes from the cat-o'-nine-tails yet. The crown of thorns hadn't dug into his scalp, nor the nails into his wrists and ankles; yet in anxiety he sweat blood.

Sometimes we feel we should be unfazed by the trials before us because our eyes are set on the good things God will bring from them. At times I've felt that my feelings of worry or fear meant that I wasn't hearing from God or I didn't have enough faith. But the fact is, we humans are hardwired (by God!) to prepare for battle or *run for dear life* when we feel threatened. It would be totally unnatural for me to feel completely calm in the face of pain, danger, heartache, or loss. How often in the Psalms we see expressed the whole spectrum of negative human emotion as David hides in caves from enemies who would kill him.

David asks for vengeance: "Pay them back for what they've done! Pay them back for their evil deeds! Pay them back for their handiwork!" (Psalm 28:4). He also begs God to stop the pain: "Please, LORD, don't punish me when you are mad; don't discipline me when you are furious. Your arrows have pierced me; your fist has come down hard on me" (Psalm 38:1-2).

David feels God has abandoned him: "How long will you forget me, LORD? Forever? How long will you hide your face from me? How long will I be left to my own wits, agony filling my heart? Daily? How long will my enemy keep defeating me?" (Psalm 13:1-2).

Despite all this crying and pleading David does, God still refers to him as "a man who shares my desires." (Acts 13:22).

Yet in the New Testament, Jesus accused His disciples of having "little faith" when their boat was caught in a nasty storm and they woke Him, shouting, "Lord, save us! We're going to drown!" (see Matthew 8:25). Why the divine mood swing? David whines for psalm after psalm and gets patted on the back, but the disciples' cry for help incites a rebuke from Jesus. I might do a little "rebuking" too if a group of people woke me up by yelling at me!

Of course, it always boils down to the heart. David cried to God with all of his capacity to feel. He expressed his anger, fear, very specific desires for revenge . . . you name it, he wasn't afraid to tell God what he thought. But at the end of the day, very often by the end of the psalm, he reminds himself that God is in control. He reminds himself that God has a plan. He reminds himself how small he is, and he reminds God that he trusts Him.

The disciples don't express much trust in God's wisdom and timing by yelling at Jesus to save them and declaring that they're going to drown. The contrast of these two

*Journal:* What are the feelings, thoughts, insecurities you're afraid to express to God?

stories teaches us a little something about the nature of emotion, how God feels about it, and how we can deal with it in His presence. Like David, we are free to express anything to God; what could we

*What could we hide from God anyway?*

hide from God anyway? Our insecurities won't embarrass our Creator. Our shame won't repulse God. We are safe. All he asks is trust. Won't we just trust God with these scary things? Won't we just see that God cares? Won't we feel how gently God handles our broken parts?

In my fear I'd asked that I be spared the pain I was facing, but again God took my hand and walked me through the fire instead of saving me from it. I could not focus on the beauty of the new life about to begin outside of me and within me, but God knew the hundreds of tearful thanks I'd offer for this, even this pain.

We got to the hospital about an hour and a half after my water broke. I was eight centimeters dilated. Two and a half hours later Ethan was born. It all happened so fast that I didn't even get a chance to see the hospital's whirlpool tub (one of the reasons I'd chosen that location), but I did it all without so much as a Tylenol, and the kind of *able-ness* I felt in that moment was unreal. I felt power. I felt as if this time I truly did something I deserved credit for.

So often I question whether people are rooting for me just because of my disability. Many times I've wondered if a pat on the back was even deserved. But that day, my having a disability did not predispose me to praise I had not earned. This was something totally unrelated to my arms. The playing field was level with all women. And I had excelled. I had never felt so *capable* in my life.

Adam held little Ethan on my chest. Ethan—*my baby*—and I looked at each other for the first time. He was perfect. I had not consulted with a geneticist prior to becoming pregnant, so in the back of my mind was that nagging little fear that my child could have AMC like me, even though there was no real reason to expect it (there have been no other occurrences in my family). But with relief I watched in wonder as my newborn son moved in ways that I never had.

❖ ❖ ❖

Through our couple of days at the hospital, I was nervous handling Ethan. This was especially true when we had visitors, or when Adam was watching. I had to learn my own ways of holding, burping, swaddling, and diaper-changing. It was like I was learning a new language, and my body spoke it haltingly. I was embarrassed at the awkwardness of my movements and the discomfort Ethan was sometimes in because I couldn't hold him in the right way. Night was my refuge. Adam stayed at the hospital with me and helped whenever I woke him, but I was excited for the nights because they were my time with my baby. I couldn't get him out of the bassinet the hospital furnished, so when it was time to nurse Ethan, I beeped a nurse and had Ethan handed to me so Adam could sleep. And, though hospital rules discouraged it, I let Ethan sleep with me in the hospital bed. The nurses came and went as Ethan and I snuggled through the night, but they never said a word.

*We humans are hard-wired (by God!) to prepare for battle or run for dear life when we feel threatened.*

When we got home, Adam was able to take two weeks of vacation to help me adjust. I was grateful for his help, and I was equally grateful when he went back to work. I needed to have one-on-one time with Ethan to get really adjusted, and the more Adam was around in those shaky first days, the less sure of myself I felt. I needed to kick into survival mode. I needed to have no one to be falling back on for help, so I could be forced to take responsibility for it all, and then I would know I could handle it.

So, Adam went back to work, and here I was with this baby, who somehow expected me to have a clue. I didn't know the first thing about babies. I had read countless books on childbirth but hadn't thought to read one on what to do after the blessed event! But even if I had, I still would've had a heck of a time figuring out the physical aspect of it. The book *Feets of Strength: Five Easy Steps to Hands-Free Child Rearing* has yet to be published.

Carrying him before he could hold his head steady was difficult for me. I learned to use my locked-under hands to hold him against me as I leaned back enough so his head would roll toward my body. I had to stay in this leaned-back position as I walked anywhere with him. Going up the steps in this posture was particularly difficult. I had a perpetual backache. Another situation to navigate was the crib. For several months he was in his Moses basket since I couldn't reach in to get him out of a crib. My parents-in-law solved that problem by generously commissioning a talented cabinet maker in the family to make doors on the front of the wooden crib, so I could open it up like a cabinet to get the baby in and out. Obstacle conquered.

Burping Ethan was also tricky to figure out but mainly because I had I'm-a-Paranoid-First-Time-Mom Syndrome. Because of the way the joints of my hands are locked in place, I can't pat Ethan's back with my palm. If I pat him on the back, it is with the inner edge of my hand (my index finger and thumb). He seemed so small and fragile, and I felt that if I tried to burp him by patting him like this, I would surely do some kind of permanent damage to his spine. So, instead, I would hold him against me and gently jiggle us both around until he burped. As you can imagine, this often ended with baby spit-up.

*You set your mind to something, and you take the thousand little steps to get there . . . one at a time.*

But sometimes you just have to take the moment that is in front of you, find some creativity, and just get through it. Were there better solutions than the ones I chose? Probably. Did I get spit up on a lot? Yeah. But I wanted to be a Mommy. It was an enormous task with way too many problems to be solved all at once or to be solved perfectly. But you set your mind to something, and you take the thousand little steps to get there . . . one at a time. There are no shortcuts to joy. There is no such thing as a "Get Fulfillment Quick" scheme. The beautiful things in life take time and practice. I can't tell you the number of times in my less-than-thirty years that I've missed out on something beautiful because I quit. I've made excuses, called in sick, and flaked out on more occasions than I'd like to recall. Until now, until I had a family, I didn't know what it meant to be really dedicated to something—to feel needed instead of needing someone else. There is now this person who relies on me (*imperfect, flaky me!*) for sustenance. In my son I see the deepest expression of faith. Whatever the circumstance, he has total confidence (at this age, at least) that Mama can make it all better. That faith, which I saw in his eyes moments after we first met, awakened something in my spirit I didn't know was there. I suddenly found myself driven to validate his faith in me.

In the two years since that August night, when I stumbled into my new life as a mother, I feel like—no, I *have been*—a different woman. There is meaning in each mundane little activity. I pick up items on the floor for safe toddling space, not just for appearances. I try to organize my time so that I can enjoy free moments with family instead of feeling guilty about other things I "should" be doing. I have rediscovered crochet, and made a kid-sized scarf to keep a small neck warm in the cold Missouri winter. I have learned to ask for help when I need it because Ethan needs me to be humble. I take the time to paint and read because I want him to see that art and beauty are important and worth our time. I am writing the book I always said I would write once I was a mother (somewhere in my heart, I always knew this would be my story to tell). I feel the reason behind all the things that used to feel like mere obligations. I feel purpose. I have seen wide-eyed trust in the eyes of my only son, and I have experienced the boundless confidence of his father, who knows full well my limitations.

I no longer feel so uncertain of what the future will bring . . . this is it. What a beautiful experience motherhood has been for me. Of course, joy, even joy so intense, rarely comes without struggle. Motherhood has provided no shortage of either.

❖ ❖ ❖

"He's getting so big," someone said to me as she held my infant son, a knowing smile on her face. "You'll be dropping him soon."

She said it in such a light-hearted, matter-of-fact tone, that I was embarrassed to feel the blood rush to my face as I gulped back my horror. As we stood there at the bottom of the staircase, it was all too easy to picture. I would be walking down the stairs, carrying Ethan down for breakfast on some otherwise happy and uneventful morning, and he would wriggle from my weak grip and go tumbling. There would be nothing I could do. What if he was seriously injured? And, even if he wasn't seriously hurt,

*Journal:* When people speak fear or doubt into your life, how do you react? Do you wish to react differently? I do! How can we respond in love while not agreeing with negativity spoken over us?

how could I ever trust myself again? Shouldn't a mother's arms be the safest place for a baby? Could I even trust myself with having another child after something like that? The thought of my sweet little boy in pain because of my disability, my shortcoming, nauseated me.

I was grateful that she was focused on my son and didn't see the wave of humiliation and terror that must have flashed across my face. I felt a pang of jealousy at how effortlessly she carried his eighteen pounds on her hip.

"Probably." I mustered a chuckle.

This wasn't the first time someone expressed such blatant doubt to my face, but it's rare enough that it always comes as a shock to me. As much as I try to steel myself to the knowledge that people doubt my ability to adapt, I didn't realize how much it would hurt to hear the doubts about how I could learn to care for my own child. There were the strangers still sending e-mails, asking how I'd carry him, change his clothes, and endless other questions. But even harder to deal with were the discouraging comments I received from friends who are close to me— who I thought knew better. Am I really a hazard to my own child? Is that how people see me?

Since I began caring for our son full-time, it seems like the constant question in my mind is, "OK, how are we going to do this?" Every new phase of Ethan's development creates a new set of challenges for us to overcome together. The moment we really nestle into a routine, he has to go and get all big boy on me and throw my nice little system out of kilter. When he was a newborn, I could bathe him in his infant tub, which fit within our bathtub. Afterward, I could lift the entire plastic tub out when we were done. (You should have seen it!) But, by the time I had figured that out, he was starting to roll around so I had to wrap him in a towel to get a good enough grip to get him out without the baby tub. Eventually, he started hating it when I did that, and I didn't have a new solution for that phase, so my solution was to have Adam give him baths! We're a team, after all. But, one night, Adam was gone on a snowboarding trip, and I had to give Ethan a bath myself. I was amazed that night when Ethan stood so still and patient, letting me wash him so thoroughly before sitting back down to play. He *never* stood still for Adam at that time. And then, when it was time to get out, he somehow knew to hold his arms very firmly to the sides so I could hook my hands under them and pull him out of the tub without a problem. I actually cried tears of relief.

That night made me realize that not only do I have God, Adam, and family standing by to help me with this child, but Ethan himself is already learning to adjust to my needs. God blessed us with a good-natured, patient child, which was exactly the temperament I needed while

I learned everything from scratch. And now we are learning and growing together. He is adapting to me, and I to him. I began to understand that night that, as Ethan gets older, he will know that Mommy is not like everyone else and sometimes she needs help.

It's very humbling to know full well that my toddler is stronger and more capable than his own mother in many ways. And it certainly complicates things when he decides to throw a tantrum and I don't even have the strength to put him in time-out if he fights me hard enough. But despite any difficulties we have, I can't be anything but thankful that he is here to keep me humble. I am so thankful that my son will have the opportunity to grow up ready to help others. What a blessing that learning tolerance will be less of a struggle for him. How glad I am that he will learn to ask for help when necessary, and to do what he can, even when he's not sure he can do it all. There will be plenty of times that having a mom with a disability will make life hard or frustrating for Ethan, but hopefully the benefits outweigh the disadvantages.

*The more challenge in one's life, the more opportunity for victory.*

As a family, we have some challenges that others do not have. But the more challenge in one's life, the more opportunity for victory, I say.

✦　✦　✦

My favorite scripture from the Bible is Psalm 23:6: "Yes, goodness and faithful love will pursue me all the days of my life, and I will live in the LORD's house as long as I live." Becoming a mother has been God's merciful answer to the prayer I didn't even know to pray. When I was younger, I was insecure enough to think I never wanted kids. I feel like this was a situation, like so many others in my life, where God's goodness hunted me down and tackled me from behind. God knew exactly what I needed and when. God knew what a joy Ethan would be to us, and even though I was afraid and unsure of myself, I can see now that in blessing me with motherhood, God's plan was best. In the past two years, I have learned more about God, myself, and people in general than I had in the previous twenty-six. I have learned that asking for help will not kill me and that independence is not all it's cracked up to be. I've learned that when I don't know what to do, I can listen for a still, small voice. I have learned that I am further from perfect than I'd ever imagined. I have learned that that's OK. And I have learned that God does not make mistakes.

God did not make a mistake when he placed me, a "special needs" baby, into the struggling marriage of two kids who knew very little about parenting and even less about disabilities. Nor did God make a mistake when He placed Ethan in such incapable arms as my own. The Creator is teaching me much in these years, but one lesson stands out in my mind as being most important for me to cling to. No matter how many moments I live that leave me feeling inadequate, or how many times, in how many ways I fail my family, they will never fall. My arms may be weak . . . *incapable*. I may see my shortcomings and know for a fact that I'm not enough, but it is not my arms that I need to focus on. Psalm 68:19 says, "Praise the Lord; praise God our savior! For each day he carries us in his arms" (NLT). My family rests in his arms. My most precious treasure rests in the most *capable* arms imaginable. I will do my very best, but where my strength fails, there God is.

*I've learned that when I don't know what to do, I can listen for a still, small voice.*

Remembering that, do I still have moments of fear? Of course. I still have nights when I break down and cry because Ethan is sick and wants me to carry him for lengths of time that I just can't accommodate. But when I can listen through the sadness in my heart, I can hear God reminding me that Ethan doesn't just belong to me. God will be what Ethan needs when I can't. My arms aren't the only ones cradling him.

# CHAPTER 10

# STRUGGLE IS NOT A FOUR-LETTER WORD

It was a typical morning for us, but isn't that how all life-altering days begin? Adam was off at work, and Ethan and I were having some breakfast at the computer desk, so I could surf the Web while spooning him his oatmeal. I was catching up on the news when I read that CNN.com was asking for readers to upload personal stories of how their families coped with having a disability in the family. The call caught my attention in such a way that I couldn't shake it. It was on my mind for days.

They weren't actually asking for stories like mine, from the disabled person's perspective, but I couldn't stop thinking that telling my story was something I should do. Surely somebody would be encouraged by seeing how we had all adapted to one another. So, a few days after I saw the call for stories, I set my little video camera up on the tripod and pushed "Record." I taped about an hour and a half of a typical morning for us, with no second takes. I let the camera roll right through me fumbling with the gazillion snaps on Ethan's pajamas and all through breakfast. I transferred the file to my laptop and edited it down to twelve minutes of footage: a little of the diaper change, the entirety of the pajama snaps (to show that things aren't as quick and easy as they may look), and a little of breakfast. I added a short introduction, where I talked about AMC and let the camera get a good look at my arms.

I watched the video through before I uploaded it. Yikes. You know how hard it is to hear your voice played back to you? How uncomfortable it is to watch yourself on tape? It was that feeling times a thousand as I watched myself turn my crooked little arms around for the camera and during the agonizingly slow minutes that passed while I dressed Ethan. This was the feeling of vulnerability, and I wasn't sure I liked it. It was the exact opposite of everything I'd worked so hard to achieve. All those years of trying to make my life look effortless, as if what I do is no big deal. As if my pain didn't matter and wasn't worth discussing. Nobody wanted to go there, right? Wouldn't everyone rather look at me and think of my strengths instead of my struggles? It had been my experience that letting people in on my difficulties only made them uncomfortable, so I pretended I didn't have any.

But if I was going to be honest about what being a mom was like, I'd have to talk about the struggles too. I scanned through the video again, considering whether to edit out some of the more awkward moments, but I found myself clicking "Submit" on CNN's website. It was done. The thing I hated most about myself was out there for the entire Internet to see. The video started something like a confession, "Hi, my name is Sarah Kovac, and I have Arthrogryposis Multiplex Congenita." Indeed, it was a confession. I confessed to myself and the world that I am flawed. I let out what felt like my most scandalous secret. I told Adam and my parents that I posted the video, but I didn't even send them the link.

> *We all feel inadequate. We all have scars we'd rather hide. We've all been rejected. We've all wished we were different.*

As I monitored my little upload, I was surprised to see it had been viewed a couple hundred times by the following afternoon. Later that day, I received a call from an unknown number on my cell phone. I answered it to be greeted by an editor at CNN. She said they were writing an article on families coping with disabilities, and she wanted to interview me for the piece. Of course I was thrilled to be a part of it. I looked forward to seeing a quotation from me in one of the upcoming articles. The following morning, a friend told me I was on CNN.com. I pulled up the site— and wow. I was *really* on CNN.com! The top headline article and photo that day featured Ethan and me, and the article contained a pared-down version of my video.

Ours was the most popular article on the site that day. Adam said he saw my video playing on CNN's TV channel as he worked at the airport. There was no hiding it now. People were finally hearing my story in its entirety—triumph and defeat alike. I had feared that it would have a polarizing effect—that if people saw how unique my daily life was, they would only see me as different, unapproachable, unlovable. But I have found the exact opposite to be true.

*Journal:* What is your story, your filmable triumph and defeat in the same moments?

What I shared that day was struggle. My struggle may look different than yours, but struggle is universal. It's something we all have in common. Sharing a struggle has the power to unify, to strengthen relationships that would otherwise be hollow.

Since that day, when I took that first step into vulnerability, I have had people send me messages that begin with something like, "I relate to your story so much. Let me tell you why . . ." We all know what it's like to feel broken, to be broken. We all know what it's like to feel shortchanged in life, to wonder why God allowed this to happen or why he doesn't fix it all. We all feel inadequate. We all have scars we'd rather hide. We've all been rejected. We've all wished we were different. But we're not. Our world is broken and full of broken people.

Pastor and writer Steven Furtick, in a popular 2011 Twitter post, told followers: "The reason we struggle with insecurity is because we compare our behind-the-scenes with everyone else's highlight reel."

We don't get a chance to experience anyone else's pain or struggle. We only see whatever they choose to show the world, which is often not quite accurate. When we choose vulnerability, it gives others the opportunity to see that they're not alone in their behind-the-scenes mess. It's difficult to be vulnerable in the culture we've created, where everyone is clawing for a slice of the pie and we measure achievement by things like money, square footage, corner offices, and education. Vulnerability, exposing our weaknesses, would only make us easy prey for everyone else who wants our job, money, and social status . . . right? Only a crazy person would let the competition in on her weak spots.

Well, I know it's not very long in the grand scheme of things, but I lived like that for twenty-five years, not letting anyone in on the dirty little secret that I struggled, and that was long enough for me to see that I did not want to continue the charade. How exhausting, to try to convince the world that everything in your life comes naturally, that you never need help with anything. If that were true for any person, that person would have no idea what a moment of victory feels like. They would not know the sense of accomplishment that comes with overcoming an obstacle that would have held them back. What joy I would lose if I had no struggles! I would contend that the more struggle a person naturally faces, the easier access that person has to joy. Opportunities for victory present themselves by the hour, in tangible ways. Gratitude comes easy to those who know they have nothing.

Maybe for the disabled, the poor, the downtrodden, the marginalized, our humbleness is just easier to feel than for the rest of humanity. When I learned to be vulnerable, I stopped clawing to be on the same level with everyone else. What I found was that everyone else was just as messed up and scared and broken as me. Some hide it better than others, some have the world fooled, and some fool them- *It's difficult to be* selves, but everyone's a mess, and *vulnerable in* everyone needs grace and help. *the culture* Maybe we who are more visibly a *we've created.* mess have an advantage; we usu- ally have to come to grips much sooner with the fact that we are imperfect and can't go it alone than someone who can hide their flaws.

Maybe all of God's promises for peace, joy, abundance, and purpose can be fulfilled in *me*. In this body. In my life, as imperfect and messy as it is. Maybe God is who and what he says he is, regardless of who and what I am.

# CHAPTER 11

# TRUE NORTH

Tomorrow. What if I knew what tomorrow would bring? Some days Ethan smiles in such a way and Adam just gets me, and I am so wrapped in the warmth of family that I am sure heaven couldn't possibly hold a candle to the beauty of this life. On those days I would stop time if I could. On those days I wish tomorrow didn't exist. But there are other times when the months are hard and cupboards are bare and patience is short and all I want to know is *when* tomorrow will come. *When* will today leave us and *when* will our lives see change? Tomorrow may bring me laughter and it may bring me pain—I can't know; I can only hope for happy days ahead. What I do know is this: the God who defines Himself as Love will be with me for every step. Through every rejection, every illness, every child growing up and moving away . . . Love will hold my hand. Love holds even these twisted hands and won't let me go. And though my world changes faster every day, children learn and circumstances shift and people are swayed like branches in a storm, I will always have a constant. I will always have a True North. I will always have God's love.

❖ ❖ ❖

Ethan and I sit in the glider and wind down for sleep in our usual way, looking out the window and talking about the stars. This is my very favorite time of day. No matter how rushed or distracted I've been, no matter how cranky or rebellious he's been, we always seem to enjoy this time together before I reluctantly tuck him into his toddler bed and we echo our way through a bedtime prayer. Sometimes we sit here, discussing the moon and trees for as long as an hour. Sometimes we drift off to sleep in each other's arms. There are few things in life I find more sacred than this daily routine of giggles, eyes squeezed shut with prayers of thanks, night sky wonders, and Eskimo kisses.

Tonight, as we sit, Ethan grows quiet and I realize he has shifted his focus away from the window and is closely examining my hands wrapped around his waist. He holds his hand next to mine to see that, while it is the same size as his, it looks very different. He watches his fingers flex and then tries to get mine to bend the same way. I sit amused as he searches for answers I still don't have. He tries to get each of my knuckles to bend like his, but they don't budge—my fingers don't bend at all. After a moment he reaches his very scientific conclusion and breaks it to me with a sigh of resignation. Ethan looks up at me with those chocolate eyes and tells me, "It's no working. Needs batteries." I love having a toddler who can make me laugh!

But I also wondered what it will be like when he starts to realize that I am a little different. I must admit, I wish he could stay naive forever in that way. I don't want him to have to think about what Mommy can or can't do. I want to make the perfect cupcakes on his birthday. I don't want him to have to deal with immature school kids or wish he had a "cool mom" like so-and-so. I don't want to embarrass him at restaurants. I don't want him to have to work through having a broken mother. I don't want him to grieve even a fraction of what I've grieved.

I don't want to be a cause of struggle for my little boy. I want life to be easy on him. But then, no good man was molded from a life of ease. I know that having a mother such as myself will bring him some hardship, but maybe he can also watch me and learn that hardship is not always bad. It can be very good. Struggle is an important part of living. Maybe having a mother like me will bring him more than hardship. Maybe revelation too. I pray that it does.

❖   ❖   ❖

As a person who likes to be prepared for anything, thinking about the future can be a little scary. I want my plan, I want it clearly spelled out, and I want to know every step it will take to get there. This second pregnancy came right on schedule, I know exactly when I'd like to start on another book, how many speaking engagements I'd like to do per month. I know that God has a plan also, and it may or may not jive with what I've got scheduled, but having ideas about the future calms me. I suppose I like the illusion of preparedness. A few years back, I learned about the concept of being a "flexible frame." I have some framework set up in my life, based on what I believe to be wisdom. But I have to keep in mind that someone far wiser than me is running the show, and if God's got something else in mind, I'm flexible.

Yes, we are now expecting our second child, a girl, shortly after this book releases. We've waited this long (Ethan will be four when his sister arrives) to add to our family because pregnancy means I

*Better instead of bitter. We each are given that choice.*

can't be there for Ethan physically in ways I was before. My arms will not be long enough to reach around a baby bump, even if my back can handle it, so no more carrying him. He is still young enough that I have to lift him fairly often, but we waited until he started becoming more independent before this full-time mom became all but useless for several months. But even now in my third trimester, I've been surprised at how much I can still do. The Lord provides.

I pray that, as he grows older, Ethan can have the grace to understand that I'm doing the best I can, even though some of his friends' moms can do more and different things. I hope he will remember how we played pat-a-cake together—with our feet. I hope he can see the special moments I give to him that no one else can. And I hope that he grows into the knowledge sooner rather than later that we all get frustrated with our parents' shortcomings, no matter how obvious or hidden. I hope that he will choose to allow my inadequacies to make him better instead of bitter. We each are given that choice.

When I think of the future, I think of joy. I think of more children sitting around our table. I think of growing even closer to Adam over time. I think of all the people I hope to meet, all the travel I hope to do as I speak. I think of Ethan growing into a handsome young man. I think of quiet days spent writing. I think of helping the discouraged, and how it moves me. I think of building a peaceful life. Don't we all?

I know what I want, and I suppose that's something . . . better than being completely without direction, right? But I also thought I knew what I wanted for a good chunk of my life before God healed me in ways I hadn't anticipated. Better ways than I *could have* anticipated. I know there will be days in the sun, when I think that life cannot get any better. I know that there will be walks through the valley, where I will cry to a God who often withholds the answers. God may not offer me answers, but always holds my hand. So what is there to fear?

Proverbs 31 speaks of a woman who "laughs at the future." It's not that she's naive. It's not that she thinks everything is going to go perfectly for her. She works hard. She is honest. She fears the Lord. In other words, she does what she can. Then, she confidently leaves the rest in

God's care. She can laugh about the future because she knows that she isn't responsible for making sure it all works out right. Just think: we don't need to be worrying about anything. We don't need to be trying to control. We don't need to anticipate every next thing, because the future isn't ours to worry about. What a relief!

*We don't need to anticipate every next thing, because the future isn't ours to worry about.*

You know enough of my story now to know that not much of my life has gone as anyone had planned. My parents weren't planning to have a child with a disability. They weren't planning to have a child at all. No one anticipated I would use my feet to do things people do with their hands. I married a man who is almost my polar opposite and had a baby before we had planned to do so. Nothing about my life has made a lot of sense, but as the one who has been living it, I can tell you . . . it's been breathtaking, in the most glorious sense of the word. My life, with its surprises, its dark days, its mountaintops, its struggle, is a beautiful place to be.

✦ ✦ ✦

Tonight, as I rock my precious boy to sleep, he'll lay in my awkward, weak arms and somehow feel at home. That is a miracle. Though I'm incapable of giving him all that I'd like to give, he will always have what he needs. Another miracle. God has given me wonderfully supportive friends and family—a community—to lean on when I have no more strength. And, the most comforting thing of all, I know that when I lay him down and watch his eyes flutter off into sleep, I know that nothing can keep my little boy from God's love, not even my own brokenness. I can rest deeply because my child, family, my life is held in God's capable arms. The arms of love. The arms of grace.

✦ ✦ ✦

*I can rest deeply because my child, family, my life is held in God's capable arms. The arms of love. The arms of grace.*

My story is probably not the most dramatic one you've ever heard. When it comes down to it, I am simply a wife and stay-at-home mom who didn't quite finish college. That's a common tale. I suppose I wrote this book and now share my story with audiences because I believe it's important for us to hear common tales from seemingly uncommon people. At first glance, my life may seem foreign because of the way I do things, but really our stories are all very similar. We all battle fear. We all wonder if we are doing enough; if we *are* enough. We have all felt stabs of rejection and we have all have let someone tell us what we're worth. We all struggle to be more than who we were, and we all need to be given (and to give ourselves) grace when we fail. The pain of loss is no stranger to any of us. We all are faced with the option of allowing pain to make us cold or to deepen the wells of our souls. Every story is unique in events, but not in experience. Not one of us is "the only one." Not one of us is alone.

❖ ❖ ❖

I hope my story causes you to rethink the people around you. Many of the details of this book have never been shared with anyone before now. No one but God knew the extent of what I was going through much of the time. I thought that suffering had to be done in silence, with a smile on my face. You don't know what kind of mess is going on behind the scenes with even the ones who seem the happiest. You don't know how much you might relate to someone who seems so different until you start talking and, more importantly, listening.

I want to thank you for listening to my story. Someday I hope to return the favor. Because every life is a story worth telling, and yours is no exception. Be encouraged as you journey through your plot. Remember my story and remember that no matter the twists and seeming dead ends, love journeys with you. May it be your North Star. When you're not looking for it, when clouds obscure the sky, it is still there. God is there. Strong and gracious and capable whether you are or not. Rest in God's capable arms, and everything else will become irrelevant. Find that knowledge, find that faith—and find freedom.

# AN INTERVIEW
# WITH MY PARENTS

When this book was nothing more than a dream in my heart, I knew I wanted my parents to contribute some of their experiences as well. It is easy to take for granted those who are closest to us, but I can't miss the glaring truth in front of me that my mother and father have incredible stories of their own. Even being so close to them, it's still clear for me to see that they are extraordinary people. I've seen them up close, in their good moments and not so good; and at the end of the day, I can still honestly say that they are my heroes. They are the ones I look up to and the standards I hold my life against. The better I've gotten to know them over time, the more impressed I've been by them both. My mother, with her resilience, creativity, and grace under pressure. My father, with his unshakable integrity and compassionate spirit. They have taught me so many priceless lessons, and imparted a treasure of lasting truth. I interviewed them and recorded their responses below so that you could get a glimpse into their minds and hearts.

**Dad:** I will never forget the moment in the delivery room as I watched you being carried away to be weighed, measured, and cleaned up before being brought back to your mother to hold (they weren't quite as concerned about bonding in those days). As the nurse carried you across the room I noticed your arms hanging from your body in what I perceived to be an unusual way. Your arms were very straight and your hands were cupped. But how could I be sure what was "normal"? I had never seen a baby at the moment of birth before and there was no indication that there was something amiss in the primitive sonogram images we had seen. While seated at your mom's right shoulder I asked a question that I was afraid to ask, but at some level already knew the answer to: "Is that normal?" I don't specifically remember the answer but it was something to the effect of "No I don't think so." That moment was the first step of a journey that started in denial and disbelief and continues today to be changed to acceptance and faith.

**Mom:** I am reminded of the first several days after we were transferred to Children's Mercy Hospital. We only had one car, so your dad would drop me off at the hospital before he made the one-hour drive to school in the morning. After work he headed for his part-time job, then he would be back at the hospital to pick me up at around 9:30 in the evening. With a few exceptions, I could only be with you when it was feeding time. Then, I could take you to a nursing mother's room while I fed you. There was a lot of down time. I would wander around the hospital between feeding times. I had to carry my sitz bath and cleaning accessories in a bag with me. Once, I was in a little room where they would allow moms to take their babies for visits. That day, there was actually another woman in there with her baby. She was telling me that her baby had to undergo open heart surgery soon after being born. But, they had been there three weeks, and they would be going home soon. I remember listening to all the scary details of their ordeal. How concerned they were when the baby was in surgery. And, how thankful they were that healing was almost complete. Soon, they could put this whole thing behind them. I smiled and said how happy I was for them. Inside, I felt so jealous. Why couldn't that be our story? It was all over for them. But for us, it was only the beginning. The physical therapy that would soon begin, I didn't even want to think about it. They said they would train us to do it. I had never done anything like this before. What if I messed up and broke some of your bones? I was scared to death.

"But anyone who needs wisdom should ask God, whose very nature is to give to everyone without a second thought, without keeping score. Wisdom will certainly be given to those who ask," it says in James 1:5.

I was constantly just hoping I was caring for you the best way possible. In your case in particular, because your condition was so rare, no one really knew. We had doctors and therapists giving us advice. But, admittedly, they were doing a lot of guesswork themselves. In a way I felt like a pioneer. It was scary. I tried to create things you could do with your feet and hands (if possible) to keep you on track developmentally.

I never saw any information instructing me how to modify anything until you were four years old, when we went to the Shriner's Hospitals for Children in St. Louis. I was always trying to think of new ways of helping you become more independent, as is any good mother of a child with special needs. Some worked, many didn't. The other very hard thing was knowing the struggles you had ahead of you, both inside and out. I worried about how you were going to find your place in the world. And prayed that your spirit wouldn't get too battered along the way. My heart ached as I thought of the pain you would endure as you would encounter people who would be thoughtless, insensitive, and cruel. And, I quickly learned it wasn't just children I had to worry about.

**Dad:** It was always a difficult thing to turn you loose and allow you to run and bike ride and roller skate like any other kid. It was always a battle in my heart and mind, but I did the best I could to allow all the freedoms possible. Many, many times it was a matter of trying to be led by God and trust in God to take care of me because there were many times that I simply could not. Of all the times that your fragile arms were injured, I don't believe they ever caused me to regret what I had allowed you to do. One main reason was that they were usually very commonplace "safe" activities. The only one that I would have changed was your choice to play soccer in an alley full of broken up and jagged concrete, which resulted in your last and worst arm break. Having said all that, every time you were hurt was heartbreaking. I can't even put into words the sick feeling in my gut when my girl was injured. As a matter of fact, with the last break, I nearly passed out when the nurses were moving your arm in a way that a "normal" arm would naturally flex. However, with your arm being locked at the elbow, they were unknowingly forcing it to bend at the break in the elbow. I feel sick even now just thinking about it. At the time I thought I would either punch a nurse or pass out. I had to leave the room so I would do neither.

**Mom:** Psalm 91:11 says, "Because he will order his messengers to help you, to protect you wherever you go." I learned to pray this scripture a lot. I reminded myself continually that you were God's child. He loves you far more than I ever could. Was I going to trust God or not? "He said to them, 'Why are you afraid, you people of weak faith?' Then he got up and gave orders to the winds and the lake, and there was a great calm" (Matthew 8:26).

I reminded myself that it did no good to worry. I needed to let it go and not think about it. Worrying was a sin anyway.

"Those with sound thoughts you will keep in peace, in peace because they trust in you" (Isaiah 26:3).

I went through this scripture and prayer cycle many times. I wanted you to experience the closest thing to a "normal" life as you could. I didn't want my fear to stand in the way of that. You deserve better than that. I wish we all could have gained the wisdom we now have without having to go through the hard times. But, that's not real life. I wish I could have understood you better. I wish I could have loved you better.

I was blessed with the opportunity to see and experience life (you and the world) in a way many others don't. To appreciate things that other people take for granted. To know and see the determination of a child who has to fight an uphill battle to achieve something. But, she hung in there and kept trying until she got it. Even if it took a really long time. Being able to celebrate that victory was a blessing, because you know what an accomplishment it truly was.

**Dad:** The thought of being the father of a child with special needs was rarely a consideration. I was just a very young dad who deeply loved his daughter. I was always so proud and honored and gratified to be the father of a daughter who, from birth, was just so special in ways that had nothing to do with her "special needs." I have always half-jokingly said that my goal as your father was "not to screw it up" because you were such an amazing person from the moment you were born. So the best thing about being the father of a child with special needs is that I got to be Sarah May Taylor's father. And there is no one's father I would rather be.

Seeing you experience physical and emotional pain and limitations that others did not have to deal with was very hard. And that *why* question is very difficult to come to terms with. Other than that, I don't know that raising you was any different from being the parent of any child. Based on what I have seen, all children have some kind of "special needs." Some of the needs are just more obvious than others. I have known some children—and adults—who appear to have no need, but in truth are the most needy. They have just become masterful at keeping those needs hidden.

**Mom:** To a mother who feels she has not been given the tools to be everything her child needs, I would say to ask God. (Again, James 1:5: "Wisdom will certainly be given to those who ask.") God is faithful. God never fails. Even if you never meet another person in your life who can relate or give advice about your situation, God can give you everything you need. Just ask. Then just watch and see all the amazing things he will do! Maybe God will bring someone into your life who has a particular interest in this or that, which just happens to be exactly what you've been looking for. God will give you all the tools you need in all sorts of ways. Just don't put God in a box. You never know how God will deliver what you need. Sometimes it isn't until afterward that you realize it was God at work making sure you had what you needed at the time. But you can trust God to help you, if you ask. God is good. He is generous. He is faithful.

**Dad:** If I could sit my twenty-one-year-old self down and tell him anything, it would be that "it is going to be OK. As a matter of fact, it's going to be better than you would dare to hope for. There will be sacrifice, pain, and hardship, but trust God. The situation you are in is no surprise to him. He knows what he is doing and it will be OK."

❖ ❖ ❖

God is good. God is faithful. God is generous. God knows what he's doing and it will be OK. This is my story and the story of my family. God is good, and it will be OK. This is our story.

# SPECIAL THANKS

I would like to extend a special thank-you from the depth of my heart, to the following individuals and organizations. They gave me the ability, the tools, and the confidence to share my story.

My husband and son

My parents, who have done far more for me / us than can be chronicled in a book

My parents-in-law, for raising a great man who changed my world

My family at Word of Life Church

Dr. Sheena Drake

Becky Castle Miller

Nancy Nelson

Linda Kosminski, M.S.W.

Melissa Cox and Lifeshots Photography

The Circle of Moms online community

The Griffon News

The wonderful souls at AMCSupport.org

As cliché as it may sound, I cannot think of my life or this book without thanking God. Even in the most difficult times, God's goodness and mercy were stalking me and ready to pounce at the first opportunity. I've done nothing to deserve the beauty his presence has brought, so all I can do is offer my most humble and astounded thanks.

And then there's you. Thank you for taking the time to journey with me. I know the road wasn't always an easy one, but I hope you found it to be rewarding. Thank you for taking the time to become part of my story, and allowing me to be part of yours.

# ABOUT ARTHROGRYPOSIS
# MULTIPLEX CONGENITA

Arthrogryposis Multiplex Congenita literally means "multiple joints crooked at birth." To be diagnosed with AMC, a person must have one or more joint contractures, meaning the joint lacks range of motion. This symptom can have any number of causes, including genetics, restriction of fetal movement, or even fetal hyperthermia/overheating (the mother suffered a lasting fever or soaked in hot tubs for long periods).

It is common for those diagnosed with AMC to suffer these stiffened joints as well as weakened/missing muscles especially in the arms and legs. Some also exhibit facial deformities, club feet, spinal cord anomalies, and even cardiac and respiratory disorders. As AMC is an umbrella diagnosis, there are hundreds of variations that can affect any part of the body. Some are so mildly affected that the disability isn't easily noticed. Others are so immobilized that they require help from aides to accomplish everyday tasks.

Despite the level of physical disability, most people with AMC have the same average IQ scores as the general population and live full, productive lives. It is non-progressive, and there is no cure. For many, mobility can be increased through physical therapy, stretching exercises, corrective surgery, and serial casting throughout childhood. New medical technologies are developed every year to improve the lives of those living with AMC.

For more information please visit www.amcsupport.org.

For other fine books, visit AbingdonPress.com

# ABOUT THE AUTHOR

Sarah Kovac was born with a rare congenital birth defect, Arthrogryposis Multiplex Congenita, which left her with barely useable arms, but she taught herself to use her feet as hands instead. The struggle to keep up physically at times was almost as defeating as her struggle to fit in socially. Over time, she learned to use her feet to type, put on makeup, cook dinner for her family, and change the baby's diapers. When Sarah responded to a call for iReports by uploading a video of a typical morning for her son, Ethan, and herself (including her diapering and feeding him with her feet), the major news story also became a major breakthrough of self-acceptance and vulnerability. After spending her life trying to be "normal,"

Sarah began to write and speak and share her story of living with AMC. Sharing that story has garnered national media attention and inspired thousands with a message of hope and love. People from all walks of life relate to the story of her desperate desire to be perfect . . . and the great healing God gave when she finally allowed herself to be "embraced by Grace."

A wife and mother, Sarah shares her personal journey of self-acceptance with audiences at churches, schools, and organizations across the country. She lives with her family in St. Joseph, Missouri.